UNDERSTANDING CULTS AND NEW RELIGIONS

Irving Hexham
and
Karla Poewe

WILLIAM B. EERDMANS PUBLISHING COMPANY
Grand Rapids, Michigan

To
EDITH BELL

Library of Congress Cataloging-in-Publication Data

Hexham, Irving.
Understanding cults and new religions.

Includes index.
1. Cults. 2. Sects. 3. Evangelicalism.
I. Poewe, Karla. II. Title.
BP603.H49 1986   291.4'2   86-16231

ISBN 0-8028-0170-6

Contents

Foreword

Conversion in any shape or form is a fascinating human phenomenon. What makes people give up and perhaps reverse their former views, and commit themselves to something quite new? Is it argument, analysis, reaction, emotional recoil, or what? Is there a common pattern?

Religious conversion is of special interest, not just to those who, like me, were consciously converted to faith in Jesus Christ and now wish to see others converted, or to those like the authors of this book, for whom the religious dimension of life is a professional academic field, but to all who take the ultimate issues of life seriously. All religions claim to provide ultimate truth and wisdom, but not all say the same thing. What, then, is going on when people become Christians, or Buddhists, or anthroposophists, or when Roman Catholics become Protestants, or vice versa? Each belief system will explain the change in terms of its own conceptions, but it is still meaningful and useful to ask how, in descriptive human terms, this process of change should be understood.

A frequent form of religious conversion nowadays is enrollment in a cult or some version of New Age religion. Distressed parents and outraged pastors often ascribe cultic recruitment to brainwashing. The present authors, however, combine their skills in anthropology and sociology to analyze the process as a product of what they call "cultural hysteria," a condition in which one feels injured and oppressed, is preoccupied with a particular life problem, and thus lies open to the appeal of confident viewpoints that present themselves as supplying the felt psychic need. Their thesis seems to me cogent and enlightening, fitting such facts as I know as well as those that their own wide-ranging exposition adduces.

To map the mechanism of conversion in this way is not, of course, to cast a vote either for it or against it, but simply to understand it as a human reality. Obviously, the value of a conversion depends finally on what one is converted to, and it is good, therefore, that the authors have noted at crucial points the difference between the myths and disciplines of the religions that they study and the corresponding features of mainstream Christianity. The net result of their labor is a book that both social anthropologists and Christian pastoral leaders will value. I am delighted to have this opportunity of introducing and commending it.

J. I. PACKER

Preface

The book is written for a specific task with a particular readership in mind. It is designed to help Christian laymen, pastors, youth workers, and theological students understand cults from an interdisciplinary perspective.

Writing the book was difficult because we recognized that many Christian readers probably lack a background in the social sciences. We proceeded, therefore, by developing our argument to take the reader from theological examples to ones from the social sciences in an effort to lay bare the framework of new religions—a framework consisting of primal experiences, new mythologies, and aspects of the great Yogic and Abramic traditions.

It is our belief that anyone wishing to talk to cult members needs to recognize that understanding must precede criticism. We believe that many of the apologetic arguments used by well-meaning Christians are undermined by a lack of insight into the lifestyle and beliefs of the people they are meant to reach. In practice such arguments tend to do more harm than good.

Our aim is to develop an understanding of cults and the people who join them—the first step toward enabling people to communicate with each other. Only when that is done can other issues be seriously considered.

In conclusion, we would like to thank the many people who helped us with our research—particularly the "cult members" who detailed their lives for us. We also thank the Social Sciences and Humanities Research Council of Canada and the University of Lethbridge for their generous financial assistance and encouragement.

IRVING HEXHAM
KARLA POEWE

1

Christian Apologetics, Deprogramming, and the Cults

Why do people join cults? Are they brainwashed or do they make a free choice? Are cults sinister groups? How should Christians react to cult members? Is it possible to talk to them meaningfully, or must we resort to coercive deprogramming? These and other questions puzzle many people. On the one hand, most of us believe in freedom of religion. On the other hand, some of us are afraid that liberal attitudes toward extremist groups may destroy our democratic institutions.

Most of us have, at one time or another, met cult members. Often it seems impossible to have a reasonable conversation with them. Faced with probing questions, Jehovah's Witnesses, Hare Krishnas, and other cult members seem to give stock answers and don't appear to take important questions seriously. To the annoyance of outsiders, cult members use unintelligible in-group jargon, and when they speak plain English, they don't use our language in quite the same way as we do.

These reactions are particularly frustrating for Christians who want to discuss theological issues. Cult members use terms such as *redemption* only to assign them meanings that are quite different from those used by Christians. Other phrases they often use, such as "go to your core" and "surrender yourself fully to the feeling from your core," resemble phrases used in the eighteenth- and nineteenth-century "encounter" styles of Pietists, such as "inward piety of believers" and "the disclosure of the interior life." Given these differences in language fashions, many Christians doubt the sincerity of cult members and accuse them of deliberately deceiving people by giving words definitions that disguise the true beliefs of the cult. The suspicion that something must be hidden has led many people to conclude that cult members are brainwashed. We believe that this reaction is wrong and that communication with cult members is possible once we understand why they joined the cult and what they believe.

CHRISTIAN APOLOGETICS

How can we understand conversion to cults? It might help to understand the mysterious by first taking a look at something more familiar: how Christians understand conversion to Christianity.

Do Christian conversion and cult conversion experiences have anything in common? Many people would contend that they do not. Many evangelical Christians maintain that their belief is reasonable while that of cult members is not. In our culture reason and nature are in alliance. What is reasonable is also thought to be natural, and so many hold that it is natural to convert to Christianity but it is not natural to convert to cults.

In addition to assuming that Christianity is more reasonable than the cults, many Christians feel that their religion is more natural because of its extensive traditions. By contrast, cults are new. Some cults derive their beliefs from several traditions, including Eastern ones. Other cults involve lifestyles that constitute pointed opposition to tradition.

The tradition to which Christians appeal, however, is not so much that of lifestyle and institutions, but of *apologetics*—the practice of defending the Christian faith against other views and criticisms by means of rational argument. This sort of defense is systematized and enshrined in the Bible. Some cults have formulated similar defenses. The Church of Jesus Christ of the Latter Day Saints, for instance, has the *Book of Mormon*. Other cults simply retreat into silence or ritual.

To justify conversion in terms of Christian apologetics narrows rather than broadens our understanding of it. It leads us to concentrate on intellectual questions about the existence of God and suggests that human experiences, conflicts, emotional turmoil, and even social and cultural upheavals are unimportant. Most apologetic approaches also ignore the fragmentation of beliefs that characterizes the modern era in a special way.

The fact is that apologetics doesn't provide the best means for understanding the conversion experience. Apologists are

principally concerned with intellectual reason alone, but sociological studies have shown that interpersonal relationships and
communal feelings play a far more important role than coldly rational deliberation in the conversion process.

THE SOCIOLOGICAL EVIDENCE

Recently a number of scholars turned their attention to questions
of having and losing faith.[1] Their findings all point in the same
general direction. They supply evidence that personal relationships are important factors leading to loss of faith or religious
conversion. Evangelists also emphasize the importance of social
ties. Paul E. Little, for instance, says "we need to discover how,
practically, we can initiate and develop friendships with non-
Christians. . . . The art of friendship has been lost by many Christians because they feel their time is being wasted when it's not in-
vested in a specifically religious activity."[2] Similarly, Rebecca
Manley Pippert's book *Out of the Salt Shaker and into the World:
Evangelism as a Way of Life* is full of stories about friendship as
the key to evangelism. She says "our sociology reflects our theology. The way we treat others reveals what we think God is like."[3]

A careful study of the Bible reveals many passages that
speak about personal relationships and friendships. Rereading
the Bible in the light of sociological theory, we can see how it
speaks to the fact that people who experience the disintegration
of social relationships find it very hard to continue to maintain
their faith. As other people grow more distant, so does God. Conversely, as faith in God grows, relationships with other people
change and are enriched. Solid human relationships seem to
make faith in the Christian God easier.

---

[1]Foremost among these scholars is Dean Hoge, author of the excellent
study *Converts, Dropouts and Returnees: A Study of Religious Change among
Catholics* (New York: Pilgrim Press, 1981). Along with David A. Roozen, Hoge
also wrote *Understanding Church Growth and Decline, 1950-1978* (New York:
Pilgrim Press, 1979) and edited *The Unchurched American: A Second Look*,
which appeared in a supplement of the *Review of Religious Research*, vol. 21
(Hartford: Hartford Seminary Foundation, 1980). See also David Caplovitz and
Fred Sherrow's pioneering work *The Religious Drop-Outs* (Beverly Hills: Sage
Publishing, 1977).

[2]Little, *How to Give Away Your Faith* (London: InterVarsity Press, 1966),
pp. 30-31.

[3]Manley-Pippert, *Out of the Salt Shaker and into the World: Evangelism
as a Way of Life* (Downers Grove, Ill.: InterVarsity Press, 1979), p. 76.

CHRISTIAN LITERATURE AND THE CULTS

Walter R. Martin has written a number of books that analyze cults from the perspective of evangelical Christian apologetics.[4] They are on the whole well-documented critical studies of the history and theology of various religious movements that deviate from orthodox Christianity, and as such they can be very useful in explaining to committed Christians the teachings of different new religions and why Christians disagree with them. But because Martin does not examine the life experiences of individuals, his works are of limited value to people who want or need to communicate directly with members of these cults. Martin equips the reader with arguments about theological systems and historical claims, but he does not provide insights into why specific individuals find cult membership attractive. The failure to address the question of what personal needs lead a person to join a new religion makes Martin's explanations too general. Moreover, because he assumes that Christianity is the only reasonable religion, he repeatedly makes the implicit suggestion that members of cults are in some sense insincere and deceptive, that cults do not really meet the needs of their members in any authentic way.

As we have suggested, there is a clear tendency among Christian scholars to dismiss the validity of the cult member's religious experience. In doing so, however, they cut themselves off from a genuine understanding of the cults. It is our contention that if we are truly to understand the nature of the cults, we must at least make an attempt to understand the social and psychological processes that cause individuals to join these religious groups. More important still, we must understand which *idiom*— Christian, psychological, satanic, or mythological—attracts individuals to cults because it is spiritually and therapeutically effective.

Some scholars argue that there is no need for us to be interested in the personal lives of cult members, that it is enough simply to learn the errors of their beliefs. After all, the New Testament authors repeatedly warn Christians against false teachers and tell them to avoid heretics. What reason could we have, then, to suggest that Christians should learn to understand and befriend cult members?

---

[4]See Martin, *The Kingdom of the Cults* (Minneapolis: Bethany Fellowship, 1965) and *The New Cults* (Santa Ana: Vision House, 1980).

It is important to consider carefully what the Bible actually says about this issue. Matthew 24:24 warns that "false Christs and false prophets will appear ... to deceive the elect." In 2 Peter 2:1 we read that "there will be false teachers among you [who] will secretly introduce destructive heresies." And 1 John 2:18 adds, "as you have heard that the antichrist is coming, even now many antichrists have come." Clearly New Testament writers both expected and warned against false teachers, prophets, and heretics, and also gave practical advice about how to deal with them. In 2 John 10 we read, "if anyone comes to you and does not bring this teaching, do not take him into your house or welcome him." And Jesus says in Luke 9:5, "if people do not welcome you, shake the dust off your feet when you leave their town, as a testimony against them." These and similar passages cause many Christians to think that they cannot possibly befriend people who belong to religious groups that hold unorthodox or non-Christian theological beliefs.

If we look at these passages more closely, however, we can see that those who are interpreting them as warnings against associating with members of cults or new religious groups are in fact taking them out of context. The New Testament's warnings about false teachers and prophets are not aimed at people *outside* the Christian church but at false teachers *within* the church. This is made clear in 1 John 2:18-19, where we read "as you have heard that the antichrist is coming, even now many antichrists have come. . . . *They went out from us,* but they were not of us." Similarly, in 2 Corinthians 11 and elsewhere Paul is clearly addressing the problem of false teachers within the church, not outside it. The comments of Jesus also fit this pattern within the context of the nation of Israel. Jesus, Paul, and other New Testament writers speak about nonbelievers outside the church in a significantly different way than they speak of false teachers within the church.

When Jesus had dealings with Romans, Samaritans, and others who were considered outcasts by his society, he did not argue about their "false" beliefs; instead, he accepted and befriended them, even at the risk of being called "a glutton and a drunkard, a friend of tax collectors and 'sinners'" (Matt. 11:19; cf. Luke 7:1-10 and John 4:7-29). Paul too dealt with non-Christians differently. He makes this explicit in 1 Corinthians 9:22, where he declares "I have become all things to all men so that by all possible means I might save some." Paul was prepared to show the nonbeliever consideration and understanding while at the same time strongly opposing deviation within Christian communities. Acts 17 gives us a vivid example of Paul's missionary technique in Athens. Preaching in the middle of the Areopagus, Paul said, "Men of Athens! I see that in every way you are very religious. For as I passed around and observed your objects of worship, I even found an altar with this inscription: TO AN UNKNOWN GOD. What you worship as something unknown I am going to proclaim to you" (vv. 22-23).

Many evangelical writers give the impression that if they found an altar to "an unknown God," they would be inclined to scorn the ignorance of the people who erected it. But Paul takes the intent of the Greeks seriously and builds his apologetic on the basis of Greek interest in religion. Not only does he respect their altar but he also quotes from the writings of the Greek authors Epimenides and Aratus, demonstrating that he had some degree of familiarity with the classical tradition.

In our situation today, Paul's example should serve to encourage us in our attempts to understand and communicate with cult members. By insisting that understanding precedes criticism and that friendship is the basis of communication, we are simply following the New Testament.

CULTS OR NEW RELIGIONS?

Defining a cult is difficult. In popular usage it has come to be equated with brainwashing and sinister manipulation, but in the history of the sociology of religion it has had a variety of meanings. James T. Richardson has produced a good definition of a cult as "a group that has beliefs and/or practices that are counter to those of the dominant culture," adding that these "beliefs and practices may also be in opposition to those of a subculture."[5] Bryan Wilson's classic work *Religious Sects* provides us with another excellent definition: "sects are movements of religious protest."[6]

Today the word *sect* is not used much to define current religious movements, largely because it is too closely associated with Christianity. New religions of our time draw on several religious

[5]See also Richardson, *The Brainwashing/Deprogramming Controversy: Sociological, Psychological, Legal and Historical Perspectives* (Toronto: Edwin Mellen Press, 1983).

[6]Wilson, *Religious Sects*, World University Library Series (Englewood Cliffs, N.J.: McGraw-Hill, 1970), p. 2.

traditions, including Eastern traditions. Nevertheless, Wilson's notion of *sect* and the current concept of *new religion* have much in common. The similarity is worth noting especially in light of the fact that much of the current literature on new religions fails to relate them to specific historical periods, cultural contexts, and particular religious traditions. When new religions are placed in these sorts of contexts, they no longer seem so new.

Richardson's definition does have several advantages. For example, it allows us to think in terms of secular as well as religious cults, to characterize certain political and artistic movements as cultic. But on the other hand, the word *cult* has become a fairly loaded term, burdened with negative connotations. Similarly, the term *sect* bears many connotations, albeit of a different sort. Because the use of these terms almost inevitably colors a discussion one way or another, we will be using more neutral terms, such as "new religious movements" and "new religions," throughout this book. It should be remembered, however, that religious movements *as movements* are not new. Break-away or independently formed religious movements have been with us for centuries. What makes them "new" at any one time has to do with their reactions to current ways of life, with their identification of specific tensions in current life, and with their specific notions of what constitutes salvation.

To call these spiritual phenomena "new religions" may be somewhat pretentious. It is so very American to give any new social or political movement born on American soil a designation implying that it is not only important and avant-garde but also the biggest and best in its class. In Austria and Germany these new religious movements (e.g., the Unification Church, the Rajneeshies, Hare Krishna, etc.) are simply called *Jugendsekte*, "youth sects." And that, in many ways, is what they are. Europe is familiar with the phenomenon of youth sects. From the late 1800s to 1913 and again between the two world wars, German and Austrian middle-class youths (children of wealthy industrialists) formed the *Wandervogel* and *Bünde*. These romantic youth movements reacted, like ours are reacting now, against the sterility of family life and affluence; they sought relief in deep personal experiences. Youth members modeled themselves after medieval scholars and rambled through the countryside. They were drawn to ideals of comradeship, community feeling, and emotional and spiritual highs as well as to Eastern philosophy.

Adolescence and young adulthood is a time of preparation

for later life, a transitional period. Some youths react against the uncertainties of this period by joining communities of others who are similarly troubled. Given the current popularity of experimenting with spiritual highs through drugs and exotic rituals, with psychic phenomena and changed states of consciousness, it is not surprising that the more successful of today's youth sects are those that focus on spiritual journeys rather than romantic ramblings.

THE ACCUSATION OF BRAINWASHING

Before we can seriously discuss conversion to new religions, we have to consider the charge that they are sinister organizations that brainwash their members. In North America and Europe many newspapers have told bizarre stories about life in new religions. Such stories depict cult members as mindless zombies. Supporting this view, ex-members speak on T.V. and radio talk shows about having been trapped by cults and subjected to sleep deprivation, protein-deficient diets, and isolation from family and friends. Similarly, the media spotlight parents who describe tragic stories about misled children they have attempted to rescue without success.

Such stories raise the question of whether brainwashing really occurs in cults. To begin to answer this question, we must consider the history of brainwashing as a theory of religious conversion.

The term *brainwashing* was first used to explain religious conversion by the British psychiatrist William Sargant, who wrote *Battle for the Mind* in 1957.[7] This book is the main source of the term as used today. Sargant argues that evangelical conversions from St. Paul to Billy Graham can be explained in terms of psychological processes that he says are akin to what was called "shell shock" during World War I. Shell shock is a psychological process that can be engineered to produce personality changes, and Sargant claims that "brainwashing" to produce a religious conversion is a similar process. By equating brainwashing with shell shock and relating both to religious conversion, Sargant was intentionally associating the conversion process with disease.

Commenting about Methodism in his conclusion, Sargant says "this is no longer the eighteenth century. Then it did not seem to matter what the common people believed because they

---

[7]Sargant, *Battle for the Mind* (London: Pan Books, 1959).

exercised no political power and were supposed only to work, not think; and because they read no books or papers. But religious conversion to fundamentalism seems out of date now; . . . the brain should not be abused by having forced upon it any religious or political mystique that stunts reason." He indicates that he considers fundamentalists—by whom he means evangelicals— to be dangerous people. He says that people like Billy Graham abuse people mentally and gain followers by brainwashing.

Since Sargant wrote *Battle for the Mind*, evangelical Christians in Britain and America have grown in numbers. As their numbers have increased, so has their political and social influence, while unfavorable criticisms of them have conversely decreased. New religions, however, continue to stand accused of brainwashing and mind-abuse—and, ironically, evangelical Christians are among the first to make such accusations.[8]

Flo Conway and Jim Siegelman have produced a variation of the brainwashing thesis, arguing that groups like the Moonies (members of Sun Myung Moon's Unification Church) use conversion techniques that place people under pressure until they *snap*, thus making personality changes possible. Evangelicals welcomed Conway and Siegelman's book *Snapping* because it was a direct attack upon the Moonies and their leader. They completely ignored a short statement on page 46 that equates the conversion practices of the Moonies with those of evangelical Christians. In their latest book, *Holy Terror* (1982), however, Conway and Siegelman press their attack upon evangelicals directly, insisting that conversion is a form of snapping or brainwashing not only among would-be new religionists but also among would-be evangelical Christians.

EVIDENCE AGAINST BRAINWASHING

We reject the brainwashing thesis not only because it represents an attack upon religious conversion generally but also because there is considerable evidence that people join new religions of their own free will.

We have four main sources of evidence about recruitment to cults. First, there are testimonies by ex-cult members who have totally repudiated the beliefs of the cult but strongly deny that they were trapped by techniques of mind control. Second, there

---

[8]See, for example, Ron Enroth's *Youth Brainwashing and Extremist Cults* (Grand Rapids: Zondervan, 1978).

are many parents, relatives, and friends of cult members and ex-cult members who seem to understand that the person they knew chose to join the cult freely. Third, there are many studies by social scientists indicating that individuals have different conversion careers, which would suggest that the conversion process is voluntary. Finally, accounts of the cult members themselves often indicate that their decision to become members in new religions followed a long search not only for meaning but also for the resolution of major life crises.

THE QUESTION OF DEPROGRAMMING

Those who assume that members of new religions are in fact brainwashed sometimes attempt to undo the brainwashing by means of a process called "deprogramming." Deprogrammers claim to "rescue" people from cults by using a variety of techniques to coerce them into renouncing their former allegiances. We have questions about both the premise and the effectiveness of deprogramming, however. Saul Levine, a professor of psychiatry in Toronto, writes that although there are many reports of individuals having been successfully deprogrammed, he has himself seen only one such case.[9] Indeed, Levine not only suggests that it is doubtful whether deprogramming helps many people; he also points out the way in which it is likely to harm the victim.

For deprogramming to work, subjects must be convinced that they joined a religious group against their will. They must, therefore, renounce all responsibility for their conversion and accept the idea that in some mysterious way their mind was controlled by others. But this idea has some very unsettling implications. If one has lost control of one's mind once, why can't it happen again? What is to prevent another person or group from gaining a similar influence? How can deprogrammed people ever be certain that they are really doing what they want to do? By its very nature, deprogramming destroys a person's identity. It is likely to create permanent anxiety about freedom of choice and leave the deprogrammed subject dependent upon the guidance and the advice of others.

Fundamentally, deprogramming denies choice and creates

---

[9]Levine, "The Role of Psychiatry in the Phenomenon of Cults," *Canadian Journal of Psychiatry* 24 (1979): 593-603. Levine defines a "successful deprogramming" as one that results in "the avoidance of the religious group for longer than a year after deprogramming, and the maintenance of a 'normal' symptom-free life outside the cult" (p. 600).

dependency. It robs people of their sense of responsibility. Instead of encouraging people to accept the fact that they chose to join a religion or realize that they made a mistake, it encourages people to deny their actions and blame others. Thus, deprogramming is not only psychologically destructive but profoundly un-Christian. The Bible repeatedly emphasizes human accountability and calls us to choose between good and evil. Deprogramming denies our responsibility to make such choices.

CONCLUSION

Once we reject the idea of brainwashing and the claims of deprogrammers, we are able to return to the question of developing an appropriate Christian response to new religions. We have already noted that although traditional apologetics is valuable because of the way it can inform Christians about the official teachings of many new religions, it is a very limiting approach when we try to understand the meaning of those beliefs as they are understood by cult members. Nor does it direct our attention to the nonrational, social, and psychological influences that lead to conversion. If we genuinely want to understand the people who have been drawn to join the new religions, we will have to consider these factors. To this task we now turn.

2

Evangelical Conversion and the Logic of Belief

THE EFFECT OF CONVERSION

Writing about his conversion, the great American philosopher and theologian Jonathan Edwards says, "after this [my conversion], my sense of divine things gradually increased, and became more and more lively, and had more of that inward sweetness. The appearance of everything was altered; there seemed to be, as it were, a calm, sweet cast, or appearance of divine glory, in almost everything."[1] Similarly, St. Paul describes the conversion experience of Christians by saying "if anyone is in Christ, he is a new creation; the old has gone, the new has come" (2 Cor. 5:17). John Wesley sums this up in his hymn "And Can It Be," in which he expresses the emotions of the convert as follows: "my chains fell off, my heart was free; I rose, went forth, and followed thee."

These descriptions, and many more, portray Christian conversion as an experience that may be aptly described as being "born again." Converts undergo a change that results in their seeing the world in a new light.

A typical reaction of Christian converts is to claim that their conversion made sense of the Bible and their life because both took on new meaning. Many Christians speak of how the Bible seemed meaningless until they were converted. Conversion, they

---

[1]*Jonathan Edwards: Representative Selections,* ed. Clarence H. Faust and Thomas H. Johnson (New York: Hill & Wang, 1962), p. 60.

12

say, removed blinkers from their eyes and enabled them to see the truth. Exactly the same claims are made by cult members. Mormons explain how the *Book of Mormon* made the Bible come alive; Moonies say the same thing about the power of *The Divine Principle*. In each case the emphasis is on the way conversion causes people to reinterpret their life in light of the teachings of a religious tradition.

Like the mother of St. Augustine, some parents of Christian converts are themselves Christians. They eagerly long for their child's conversion. More often, however, a Christian's parents are not Christians. Such parents frequently react to the conversion of their child with confusion or horror. To them it seems that their child has gone mad. Often they do what they can to discourage their offspring's newly found faith. Worst of all for the unconverted parents, spouses, and friends of a new convert is the sense that they can no longer understand the person. Suddenly the convert's world has changed. It is shaped by a new outlook, dominated by new goals.

Outsiders find it very difficult to understand and appreciate evangelical Christianity. Many psychiatrists contend that Christians are deviants who need help. The common psychiatric explanation of conversion is that converts are passive, dependent people who seek an "easy out" or a "crutch." Christian attitudes (especially sexual attitudes) are commonly held to be "unhealthy," and many embittered people are quick to blame Christianity for all their problems. Non-Christians often react to Christianity in essentially the same way that outsiders, both Christian and non-Christian, react to new religions.

UNDERSTANDING NEW RELIGIONS

Reflection on the biblical understanding of conversion ought to help us understand the conversion process of members of new religions.[2] Examples of well-known converts to Christianity throughout the history of the church should also help. Unfortunately, Christians are often unwilling to explore the worldviews of other people. Many Christians have developed a tunnel vision, refusing to look at the world except through Christian eyes. It is

---

[2]In addition to the discussion in the text, see Robert O. Ferm, *The Psychology of Christian Conversion* (London: Pickering & Inglis, n.d.), and Owen Brandon, *The Battle for the Soul: Aspects of Religious Conversion* (London: Hodder & Stoughton, 1960).

important to remind such people that new religious movements are no more incomprehensible than foreign cultures or, indeed, Christian conversion. With a little effort, they can be understood.

To the outsider, the world of the believer is an alien culture. The easiest and safest reaction to an unfamiliar worldview of this sort is simply to say that it makes no sense, that it is irrational. Attempting to understand those unlike us entails looking closely at our own beliefs and way of life, and many people find that a threatening prospect. Modern philosophy and anthropology can help us understand the threats and benefits we encounter when we immerse ourselves in an alien belief system or culture.

It is easy to dismiss members of new religions on the grounds that they joined because they ceased to think, but this assumption is unwarranted. In his classic anthropological study *Witchcraft, Oracles, and Magic among the Azande,* E. E. Evans-Pritchard showed that popular European reactions to African witchcraft ignore the psychology and logic of this belief system.[3] Europeans fail to recognize that witchcraft is a *rational* way of dealing with the *irrational* forces of envy and hatred. As explanation, witchcraft is incompatible with European thought; as symptom of social disease, it is real.

Witchcraft beliefs, although scientifically false, follow a recognizable logic. Once the logic of witchcraft is understood, a person can predict the reactions of people who believe in it. And an acceptance of the reality of witchcraft as both symptom and belief system is essential for anyone wishing to understand the traditional Azande.

In a similar way, anyone who wants to communicate effectively with members of new religions must enter their thought world. It can be done only by recognizing the logic of their beliefs. This is not to say that entering other thought worlds involves abandoning one's own or accepting the beliefs of the religion in question as beyond criticism. But it does call upon the investigator to show genuine respect for the other person's beliefs and a willingness to risk understanding them. It demands, in short, that both the Christian and the member of the new religion become aware of what it is exactly that they believe. Not infrequently, such an encounter will lead to a better understanding of both themselves and each other.

-----

[3]See Evans-Pritchard, *Witchcraft, Oracles and Magic among the Azande* (London: Oxford University Press, 1937).

THE LANGUAGE OF FAITH

The philosophical insights of the Austrian philosopher Ludwig Wittgenstein can help us understand the language and beliefs of new religions. In his *Philosophical Investigations* he discusses what he calls "language games," using that phrase "to bring into prominence the fact that the speaking of language is part of an activity, or of a form of life."[4] In essence, he argues that various "language games" or "forms of life" exist within society, each having its own intelligibility and internal coherence.

According to Wittgenstein, religion constitutes one such language game. Those who understand it hold the key to the community of believers. The British philosopher Peter Winch developed Wittgenstein's notion of understanding further, suggesting that "the notion of intelligibility is systematically ambiguous. . . . Its sense varies systematically according to the particular context in which it is being used."[5] Yet another philosopher, D. Z. Phillips, emphasizes the importance of participation as well as contextualization. In his book *The Concept of Prayer*, for example, he states that the "believer must be a participant [because] . . . to know how to use the language is to know God."[6]

The importance of context and participation for religious language was also recognized by Paul Tillich, who wrote that "faith needs its language, as does every act of personality." He argued, in other words, that the language of faith is "created in the community of believers."[7] Evangelical Christians reacted strongly against Tillich's assertions. Many evangelical writers accused him of being an atheist. Others more charitably said that whatever his beliefs, his written works are definitely un-Christian. But no matter what we think of Tillich's theology, we must acknowledge his profound insight into the workings of religious language.

Both Tillich and Wittgenstein point out that religious communities create and use their own languages and that believers find meaning within these languages. To the outsider, the language of the religious community is likely to sound meaningless and confused, but to the believer it represents a systematically co-

---

[4]Wittgenstein, *Philosophical Investigations*, 3d ed., ed. Kenneth Scott (New York: Macmillan, 1963), p. 11e.

[5]Winch, *The Idea of a Social Science and Its Relation to Philosophy* (London: Routledge & Kegan Paul, 1958), p. 18.

[6]Phillips, *The Concept of Prayer* (New York: Schocken, 1966), p. 50.

[7]Tillich, *The Dynamics of Faith* (London: Allen & Unwin, 1957), p. 24.

herent way of understanding. How to convey this understanding to outsiders is a key problem.

Because religious or spiritual experiences are highly individual and potentially idiosyncratic, language plays another important role. It socializes and makes public what would otherwise remain highly subjective and noncommunicable. Language is used in similar ways in nonreligious groups as well. Paul Hellas, for example, points out that the language of residents of Marin County, California, transforms extreme individualism into a social phenomenon. The "psychobabble" that these individuals use to describe their experiences makes them feel that they are part of "a group mind."[8]

RATIONALITY AND BASIC ASSUMPTIONS

The intimate tie between language and the community of believers suggests that we may not be quite so rational as we generally suppose ourselves to be. Most of us in the Western world have grown up assuming that sensible and intelligent people believe things because they have been proved to be true, that the world operates in terms of reason. We assume that there is only one objective truth and that we can determine that truth by employing inductive, deductive, or abductive reasoning. Not just modern science but also much of Christian thought follows these principles of reasoning. We tend to reject other ways of building symbolic universes as irrational.

Unfortunately, the rational model of the world is not as straightforward as most of its advocates would have us believe. Both Wittgenstein and Tillich offer alternative ways of understanding rationality. And however much talk about "alternative rationalities" may alarm many people, as one studies alternative systems of secular or sacred thought, it becomes clear that reasonable individuals deduce the workings of their universe from a variety of different assumptions. People build on these assumptions because they presume them to be self-evident, and presuming them to be self-evident, they rarely question them. Yet we find that what is "self-evident" for one person may well not be self-evident for another. And of course the viability of any given sym-

---

[8]Paul Hellas, "Californian Self Religions and Socializing the Subjective," in *New Religious Movements*, ed. Eileen Barker (New York: Edwin Mellen Press, 1982), p. 79.

bolic universe depends on these assumptions. So long as the Azande, for example, believe in the active intervention of the dead in the lives of the living, their sacred beliefs centered on the worship of ancestors or other unseen forces remain altogether understandable.[9]

THE DISCARDED IMAGE

Since new religions typically arise in reaction to the prevailing worldview, it will be worthwhile for us to take a closer look at the nature of the scientific worldview that prevails in our culture and to assess its—and our—place in the larger global cultural context.

As C. S. Lewis points out in his book *The Discarded Image*, and Arthur O. Lovejoy in his *Great Chain of Being*,[10] the nature of medieval thought is vastly different from our modern Western worldview. Essentially, it was assumed in the premodern West that the earth was the center of a universe created and governed by God through the agency of angelic beings. In this creation everything had its allotted place, from the lowliest single-cell organism to the loftiest archangel. All things, including human society, were presumed to be ordered by God on a hierarchical scale that reflected a cosmic structure and divine purpose. The earth was held to be a fallen realm of death and decay at the center of the universe. Above the earth were the heavenly, changeless realms of perfection and angelic beings. Below the earth was hell for sinners and fallen angels. On earth God maintained order through the authority of his church and duly appointed political rulers, who owed their place to the will of God.

This premodern worldview, or "myth," has of course been largely discarded and replaced by new myths. As a result of the much greater cross-cultural contacts of today's world, the new myths, which we will discuss later, are colorful mosaics incorporating symbols from all of the world's principal spiritual traditions.

---

[9]For a popular discussion of these problems from a Christian perspective, see Francis A. Schaeffer, *The God Who Is There* (London: Hodder & Stoughton, 1968). Schaeffer popularizes ideas derived from Herman Dooyeweerd's *New Critique of Theoretical Thought* (Philadelphia: Presbyterian and Reformed, 1953). In his various writings, Dooyeweerd presents an exhaustive discussion of the problem of rationality from an evangelical Christian perspective.

[10]Lewis, *The Discarded Image* (Cambridge: Cambridge University Press, 1964); Lovejoy, *The Great Chain of Being* (New York: Harper & Row, 1960).

THE MAKING OF THE MODERN WORLD

In the sixteenth century the Christian God-centered vision of life was shattered by a series of events and new ideas that gave birth to the modern world. Copernicus challenged the notion that the earth was the center of the universe. More significantly, Galileo used his telescope to show that the heavens, the moon and planets, were material realms subject to change and decay just like the earth. The cosmological basis of the old order was dealt a death blow from which it never recovered.[11]

Martin Luther (1483-1546) and John Calvin (1509-1564) cast serious doubt on the claims of the Roman Catholic Church and thus undermined the intellectual authority of the old order. By insisting that all people read the Bible for themselves and act according to their conscience as directed by Scripture, the Reformers initiated serious questioning of the social order. Questioning began with religious institutions but soon embraced secular structures as well. Once the Roman Catholic Church lost its religious authority, secular institutions that it legitimated were open to criticism. Calvin's followers the Puritans began criticizing church government and ended by doubting the judgment of kings.

The rapid development of religious criticism into philosophic and political criticism is discussed in numerous works on the sixteenth and seventeenth centuries. Michael Walzer's *Revolution of the Saints* and Christopher Hill's *Intellectual Origins of the English Revolution* do a particularly good job of vividly illustrating the change in basic assumptions.[12] Thomas Kuhn addresses the theoretical importance of changing assumptions and paradigms in his classic study *The Structure of Scientific Revolutions*.[13] These works among others show how a view of the world as ordered and hierarchical as that which had existed since Roman times was replaced by a new worldview based on radically different assumptions. Democratic thinking replaced hierar-

---

[11]See Marie Boas, *The Scientific Renaissance: 1450-1650* (London: Collins, 1962); and A. Rupert Hall, *From Galileo to Newton: 1630-1720* (London: Collins, 1963).

[12]Walzer, *The Revolution of the Saints: A Study in the Origins of Radical Politics* (Cambridge: Harvard University Press, 1965); Hill, *The Intellectual Origins of the English Revolution* (Oxford: Oxford University Press, 1965).

[13]Kuhn, *The Structure of Scientific Revolutions*, 2d ed. (Chicago: University of Chicago Press, 1970).

chical authority, and the vision of nature ordered by spiritual beings gave way to a universe governed by God's law. A renewed Christian ethic, based on a perception of God as transcendent and exemplary, enabled the unleashing of human creative powers. The anxieties about the envy and jealousies of one's neighbors generated by belief in witchcraft were conquered by the moral message of Christianity.

SCIENCE AND REASON

Isaac Newton (1642-1727) believed that God ordered nature through divine Law. His system of natural philosophy gave a strong impetus to the development of ideas about the laws of nature. Newton's scientific work led to the emergence of what became known as the Newtonian worldview, which pictures the universe as a closed system, rather like a mechanical toy or watch, regulated by natural laws. Such a worldview suggests that it is the task of science to discover natural laws by empirical investigation.

Newton was deeply religious and studied Scripture along with the natural world. He did not find contradictions between the truths he discovered by scientific investigation on the one hand and study of the Bible on the other. His successors, however, increasingly rejected the Bible as a means to attaining knowledge; they valued the truths uncovered by empirical investigation more than the truths received from special revelation. In time, reason came to replace revelation as the accepted source of true knowledge, and natural philosophy grew into modern science.

By the middle of the nineteenth century, technological advances and medical discoveries seemed to confirm the value of science and reason. Religion was progressively relegated to the realm of personal devotion and ethical beliefs within the larger framework of an essentially rational, ordered, and nonsupernatural universe. As they developed, modern school systems increasingly sanctioned the assumptions of the Western scientific worldview while discrediting other views.[14]

Although various individuals heading different intellectual movements revolted against the domination of scientific rational-

---

[14]On this, see Alan Richardson, The Bible in the Age of Science (London: SCM Press, 1961); and Hall, The Intellectual Origins of the English Revolution.

ism, state educational systems ensured its survival. Since the mid-1960s, however, these assumptions have come under increasing attack. And some of these attacks, as we shall see, have been led by inventors of new religions and their adherents.

CHANGING ASSUMPTIONS OF MODERN SOCIETY

Today the basic assumptions of Western society are threatened by change. Quantum theory and other scientific advances have led many scientists to abandon notions of a closed and mechanistic universe. Instead of talking about natural laws, scientists are content to operate in terms of generalizations in the form of statistical probabilities.[15]

The general public, however, is less comfortable with the uncertainties of these generalizations. People are not satisfied with the world as depicted by empiricism. They rebel against viewing the world as a mechanism composed of a multitude of parts that seem to grow more numerous and less comprehensible as research progresses. They rebel against a view that reduces even social reality to biochemical processes. One senses a craving for a new holism. The response of some social scientists is to produce a new *scientific* holism that not only leaves the social and cultural context intact but shows its influence on human well-being, even physical health. Likewise, some religious practitioners have endeavored to produce a new *religious* holism that promotes a new spiritual or religious ideology to "put right" the imbalance and disharmony that result in so many forms of social disease.[16]

The danger of holism is that it can easily be transformed into totalitarianism. German National Socialism in the 1930s and '40s remains the most potent recent example of a holism gone awry. National Socialists intended to cure German "soul sickness" by promoting a new worldview that united the spheres of science and spirituality into a single politico-religious system of thought and practice.[17]

---

[15]See Banish Hoffmann, *The Strange Story of the Quantum* (London: Penguin, 1960).

[16]See Paul C. Reisser, M. D. Teri, and John Weldon, *The Holistic Healers: A Christian Perspective on New-Age Health Care* (Downers Grove, Ill.: InterVarsity Press, 1983); and Fritjof Capra, *The Turning Point: Science, Society and the Rising Culture* (New York: Simon & Schuster, 1982).

[17]See James M. Rhodes, *The Hitler Movement: A Modern Millenarian Revolution* (Stanford: Hoover Institution Press, 1980).

The general discontent with modern science being felt throughout much of our modern Western society and the sorts of measures that are being taken to correct it raise two questions that are especially important in the context of this book. First, is a totalitarianism that is in its initial impetus political in nature different from one that is in its initial impetus religious? And second, is the content of Christianity more conducive to furthering human freedom than that of new religions? We will be looking for answers to these questions at length later in the book.

OVERVIEW OF THE CHANGES TO MODERNITY

As the roles of science and religion have changed along with the prevailing worldview in Western culture through the centuries, so the perception of the nature of the human being has changed. We have perceived ourselves differently in each historical period. In the thirteenth century the paradigm was Spiritual Man. By the sixteenth century this image had changed to Intellectual Man. In the eighteenth century the image of Economic Man became popular. This image persists even today, although it is somewhat tarnished. Importantly, we have recently developed a considerable variety of images to define ourselves. Existential philosophy introduced the image of Irrational Man, Marxism that of Social Man, National Socialism that of Heroic Man, the new mythology that of Experiential Man, and the new science that of Holistic Man.[18]

The profusion of images has much to do with the mobility and fluidity of modern life. People have shown themselves willing to give up the security associated with adopting a single identity for life in order to gain the flexibility and choice afforded by a less rigidly defined identity—even at the cost of some uncertainty and anxiety. Robert Jay Lifton argues that the prevailing modern image is that of *Protean Man* (Proteus being the Greek god who can change his identity at will).[19]

Of course, not everyone is content with exchanging security for flexibility. Scholars argue that some people join new religions because they are distressed and dissatisfied with the prospect of Protean Man. It seems clear that at least some young people have

---

[18]See Peter Drucker, *The End of Economic Man: A Study of the New Totalitarianism* (New York: John Day, 1939), and *The Future of Industrial Man: A Conservative Approach* (New York: John Day, 1942).

[19]Lifton, "Protean Man," *Partisan Review* 35 (1968): 13-27.

been drawn to the conservative Unification Church, for instance, precisely because it stands for commitment. They know implicitly, if not explicitly, that making choices, remaining true to those choices, and living with the consequences of those choices have much to do with becoming a person and developing character. A different sort of reaction against the prevailing values of our society is evident in some of those who have joined the Rajneeshies. They concur with the larger culture in valuing flexibility in attitudes and experiences but they avoid our culture's emphasis on extreme individualism by living in a community with others who share their views. In this kind of Utopian movement, the individual can enjoy the benefits of "self-actualization" without paying the cost of social isolation.

We have noted just a couple of the attitudes that distinguish contemporary Western culture from its counterparts in earlier eras. There are many such attitudes and values that pointedly distinguish many of today's new religions from the religious movements and sects that arose several centuries ago. In those earlier movements, there was on the whole a much more pronounced emphasis on the spiritual value of such things as suffering, sorrow, duty, effort, perseverance, decision, commitment, and in general asceticism. Current movements, in contrast, tend to place greater emphasis on peak experiences, euphoria, "flowing with the stream," surrender, adaptability, fluidity, tentativeness, and in general self-actualization. It is not that the ascetic attitudes no longer exist; it is rather that they have on the whole become unfashionable and suspect. It is no longer generally assumed that the sort of self-sacrifice involved in, say, voluntarily living a life of poverty or even seeking martyrdom will bring spiritual exultation.

Examples of the new attitudes are clearly evident in the writings of Abraham Maslow, an individual who has deeply influenced the current religious ethos and contributed to the California "psychobabble" phenomenon. Maslow talks about a new brand of psychology, the psychology of the fully evolved and authentic self. It should parallel if not replace, he says, the "psychopathology of the average." In his book *Toward a Psychology of Being*, Maslow dismisses European existentialists for "harping" on "dread, anguish, and despair," for being "high I.Q. whimperers on a cosmic scale." These whimperers should have known, argues Maslow, that the discovery of identity is *exhilarat-*

ing and *strengthening* and comes from experiences of *joy* and *ecstasy*.[20]

But Maslow, an American in California, simply overlooks much of history and the living conditions in the Third World. He ignores the fact that much of European history *was* grim and anxiety-ridden. It shaped Europeans as surely as the extreme conditions and cultural despair of much of the Third World shapes much of the world's population now. He also overlooks the fact that people—St. Francis of Assisi, for example—have voluntarily assumed poverty and managed to transform it into freedom, even frivolity.[21]

When we study the singular emphasis on joy, peak experiences, and exultation of some new religions, such as the Rajneeshies, we cannot but agree with G. K. Chesterton, who wondered whether religion, when simplified "all to a single idea," does not "so lose the breadth and balance of Catholicism."[22]

Nevertheless, ours is a different world. It is inevitable that new forms of self-perception and new attitudes should accompany the spirit of our times. Some new religions, perhaps more freely than many of us individually, acknowledge the shift from the predominance of a mechanical model of the universe to the model of an open universe, from the predominance of Christianity to the ascendance of other religions, from a focus on God to a focus of a more generalized spirituality, from Western cultural triumphalism to cross-cultural accommodation, from Economic Man to Holistic Man, from catholicism to internationalism. In this sense, however, the new religious movements of today, like those of times past, share at least one major function: they stand as a corrective to astonish and awaken the world.

---

[20]Maslow, *Toward a Psychology of Being* (New York: Van Nostrand-Reinhold Books, 1968).
[21]See Victor W. Turner, *The Ritual Process: Structure and Anti-Structure* (Chicago: Aldine Publishing, 1969).
[22]Chesterton, *St. Francis of Assisi* (1923; New York: Image Books, 1957).

3

The New Mythology:
Mythological Fragments

What Maslow, in the context of Western modernity, calls peak experiences, others, in the context of non-Western traditions, call primal experiences. Traditional societies mediate the effects of vivid primal experiences through the use of rich mythologies that enable individuals to accept and seemingly understand their psychic condition. But modern man suffers from a fragmentation of belief that often leaves those who have primal experiences without any acceptable means of resolving the conflicts associated with primal realities.

In medieval Europe, people who encountered the primal saw visions of saints and the Virgin Mary. Hindus in India see the gods Krishna and Rama, Buddhists meet Bodhisattvas, and Muslims share visions of God. By contrast, in industrial society, people encounter raw experiences without readily available imaginative frameworks to give the experience content and meaning.

Industrial society has no body of shared beliefs, no common mythology. Its members hold onto a collection of disconnected beliefs and are vaguely familiar with fragments of many myths. The advantage that some new religions have in this situation is that they possess powerful integrated mythologies that accommodate primal experiences.

The mythologies of new religious movements are created out of numerous disjointed myths found in society generally. By weaving these unrelated myths into coherent wholes, new religions create a sense of continuity with society. Through the use of traditional myths, they are able to give themselves an apparent historical depth that legitimates their claims to be the carriers of a high culture.

If we are to appreciate how myths are manipulated by the new religions, it is important that we reflect on the function of myth in society. In common speech, to call a story "a myth" is to say that it is untrue. This understanding of the meaning of *myth* dates back to the Greek philosophers of the third century B.C. and was popularized by Enlightenment thinkers in the late eighteenth century. A good example of such a rationalist approach to myths can be found in the works of Plato. In his dialogue *Euthyphro*, Plato depicts his mentor Socrates discussing the traditional myths of Greek society with a young man who firmly believes they are true. By a series of clever questions and leading arguments, Socrates soon establishes the contradictory nature of the traditional mythology and so casts doubt on the veracity of the myths themselves. The eighteenth-century deist Tom Paine similarly cast doubt on biblical stories in his book *The Age of Reason*, dismissing them as false myths.

The skeptical understanding of myths as stories that are essentially untrue permeates rationalist thought. People in our culture find it difficult to think of myths as anything other than fairy tales. This dismissal clouds their awareness of the way in which myths color their thoughts and actions. To understand the function of myths in the lives of individuals and in society as a whole, we must suspend our skepticism about their truth value.

Myths are stories that serve specific social functions. They enable members of different societies and subgroups within societies to understand themselves and their world. As anthropologist John Middleton puts it, "a myth is a statement about society and man's place in it and in the surrounding universe. . . . Myths and cosmological notions are concerned with the relationship of people with other people, with nature and with the supernatural."[1]

What makes a story a myth is not its content, as the rationalists thought, but the use to which the story is put. The success of the myth depends upon the belief of people in the truth of the story and the relevance of the way it interprets their social reality.

---

[1]Middleton, in *Myth and Cosmos*, ed. John Middleton (New York: Natural History Press, 1967), p. x.

Questions of historic, philosophic, or any other verifiable truths are unimportant in the creation of mythologies. What matters is the power of myths to inspire belief and to enable believers to make sense of their experiences.

Once accepted, a myth can be used to ennoble the past, explain the present, and hold out hope for the future. It gives individual and social life meaning and direction. This ability to guide action distinguishes myths from legends, folk tales, and other stories. In short, myths have the power to change lives and shape societies.

The validity of individual myths is enhanced when they are incorporated into larger or related myths. In many societies, myths are officially sanctioned through public recognition. Thus in medieval Christian Europe many myths, such as those about King Arthur and the Holy Grail, were publicly recognized. In Hindu society, myths about Krishna and other deities are given sanction in all areas of life. Christian societies have traditionally given official recognition to Christian mythologies, Islamic societies to Islamic mythologies, Buddhist societies to Buddhist mythologies, pagan societies to pagan mythologies. In other words, the dominant religion in any given society typically provides its members with a powerful mythology that receives full recognition and social sanction.

Christians tend to be reluctant to admit that myths have important functions in society and that Christianity has provided Western society with official myths for almost two thousand years. They tend to feel that Hindu stories about Krishna are clearly ahistorical myths and therefore untrue, whereas Bible stories are historical narratives and therefore true. Such reasoning has nothing to do with the status of the Bible stories as myth, however: the historical truth value of myths derived from biblical stories is not at issue. The point is that in Europe and North America, biblical stories have informed or functioned as myths and thus have had great power to mold society and give it direction.

The questions that trouble many Christians—"Did Jesus rise from the dead?" "Was the tomb of Jesus empty on the first Easter morning?" "Are miracles possible?"—are questions of historic and theological truth and as such are in a completely different category than questions about the role such stories have played as myths in society. The historical truth or falsity of myths has no real bearing on their being able to function as myths. When we talk about biblical stories providing society with powerful myths, we are not discussing their truth claims. We are simply observing that particular stories affect those who believe in them and have important consequences for the quality of social life.

Speaking of the power of myth, Northrop Frye has noted that "certain stories seem to have a peculiar significance: they are stories that tell a society what is important for it to know, whether about its gods, its history, its laws, or its class structure." Commenting on modern society, he says, "in Western Europe the Bible stories had a central mythological significance of this kind until at least the eighteenth century."[2] By a "central mythological significance," Frye means the power of certain myths to provide a general mythological framework that incorporates all the other myths to be found in a given society.

From the time of St. Augustine in the fifth century to the Enlightenment in the eighteenth century, biblical stories provided the framework of European mythology. Other myths found in different parts of Europe were Christianized and incorporated into this framework. Stories such as that of Beowulf and Islandic, Norse, and Germanic sagas were reinterpreted and given Christian meanings. The legend of King Arthur and the quest for the Holy Grail is a striking example.[3] The thrust of incorporation may take one of two directions. When Christianity is on the advance, pagan myths are Christianized; when it is in retreat, Bible stories are mythologized, sometimes into foreign myths.

Since the end of the eighteenth century, biblical stories have ceased to provide the central mythology of Western society. Owing to the skepticism of the Enlightenment and nineteenth-century freethinking, most Westerners no longer find in Christianity the basic imaginative and mythological framework by which they understand their place in the world. True, many people still profess to be Christians. But on the whole, Christian belief has been reduced to the realm of private spirituality, and as a result Western social mythologies lack a strong Christian content at both their popular and official levels.

Certain subgroups within modern society still retain a strong element of Christian mythology in their understanding of

---

[2]Frye, *The Great Code: The Bible and Literature* (New York: Harcourt Brace Jovanovich, 1981), p. 33.

[3]R. F. Treharne shows how this body of pre-Christian stories was successfully incorporated into a Christian framework to produce a powerful medieval mythology; see *The Glastonbury Legends* (London: Sphere Books, 1971).

life. It is also true that "Christian values" often inform law and other official elements within different Western societies. But nowhere today do we find biblical mythology providing both the popular and official myths of modern industrial society.

Once we realize that myths play an important role in social life and that modern Western society no longer embraces its traditional Christian mythology, we might well ask whether other mythologies have replaced the biblical framework. The answer seems to be that Western democracies are experiencing a mythological vacuum; they do not seem to have any officially sanctioned central myth. Biblical myths would appear to have been replaced by a large number of fragmented myths circulating among different subgroups without the benefit of an integrative central mythology. We make this observation with some caution, however, because we shall argue later that a central mythology does, in fact, exist, although it has not received official sanction outside of the new religions. But before we describe this emerging mythological framework, we must first identify the major mythological fragments that are currently popular.

TYPES OF MYTHOLOGICAL FRAGMENTS

We can identify seven types of common mythological fragments: prophetic myths, myths of disembodied intelligences, myths of fortune, neopagan myths, healing myths, pseudoscientific myths, and technological myths. We shall discuss each of these in turn.

Prophetic myths involve beliefs about the ability of individuals, with or without the help of certain devices, to foretell the future. The considerable recent growth in the popularity of this type of myth can be seen in the fact that in 1940 only 200 daily newspapers in America carried horoscopes, whereas today over 1,750 daily newspapers print them. In addition, there are at least 10,000 full-time and 175,000 part-time astrologers presently working in America alone.

One of the most popular of these astrologers is Jeane Dixon, who has successfully manipulated the media to gain a considerable following. Her claims to predict events accurately are regularly reported, but her failures, such as her 1979 prediction that President Carter would "suffer a church-related assassination attempt," are overlooked.

Equally popular and questionable are the writings of the late Edgar Cayce. His predictions were appropriately vague, making it difficult to subject them to the canons of disproof. His prediction in the 1940s that "sometime between 1958 and 1998" San Francisco would be destroyed by an earthquake did little to enhance his reputation except with the most gullible.

Even more difficult to refute and more clearly mythological are the so-called "prophecies" of the medieval mystic and court astrologer Nostradamus. His cryptic writing style and symbolic language allow one to read almost anything into his works, making possible both wild and plausible predictions.

At a more personal level, teacup readings, tarot cards, the I-Ching, and other techniques of divination provide countless individuals with what they take to be experiential confirmation of their belief in prophetic myths. More importantly, the combination of high-profile media prophets like Dixon and the writings of Cayce, Nostradamus, and other "recognized" seers lends credence to the claims of local diviners, while personal divination reinforces belief in the better-known figures. Such positive feedback between local and media prophets mutually reinforces their respective prophecies, making both seem plausible to anyone who is predisposed to believe in them.

Myths of disembodied intelligences include stories about ghosts and poltergeists, spiritualism and belief in incorporeal beings. Some individuals who have primal experiences explain them in terms of such phenomena because ghost stories and the like are familiar to most people in our culture. Press reports of hauntings, poltergeists, and other psychic events increase the climate of belief. Suggestibility is further heightened by such films as *Rosemary's Baby, The Exorcist*, and *The Omen*.

The resistance of many people to explaining primal experiences in terms of the occult is further reduced by exposure science fiction films and television series (e.g., *Star Trek*) and by science fiction novels generally. When *Star Trek* first appeared in the 1960s, belief in the occult was at a low ebb. Projecting the story into the far distant future and appealing to an evolutionary and, therefore, scientific justification, enabled the writers of *Star Trek* to introduce legitimately disembodied intelligences and other strange happenings. If these ideas had been placed within a spiritual framework or made to happen in contemporary society, viewers would have rejected the ideas as ridiculous. But given the futuristic orientation and evolutionary justification, such ideas were accepted as "scientific" and "possible in time."

Once people accepted such things as possible within the

framework of *Star Trek*, it was an easy and logical step to utilize similar ideas in other contemporary stories. It also became easy to make the imaginary shift from extraterrestrial intelligences to spirits and demons. Contemporary occultism owes a good deal of its popularity to pseudoscientific ideas.

In science fiction writing proper, the shift from hard science to fantasy took place in the mid-1960s. The futuristic scientific interests of older writers such as Isaac Asimov gave way to the cultural and intellectual relativism of younger anthropologists such as Ursula LeGuin. LeGuin and other New Wave authors offer us worlds inhabited by spirit beings motivated by magical spells rather than Martians, spaceships, and ray guns.

Myths of fortune are beliefs in luck. More than the other mythological fragments, these myths point to an increasing belief in a magical and occult universe within Western culture. Belief in luck has always existed in Western society of course, but this general belief was Christianized, and it rarely affected a majority in any given society. Luck was more often associated with gamblers and thus was officially scorned by society. But with the growth of the new mythologies, luck has returned to dominate the attitudes of a large number of people.

In her book *And I Thought I Was Crazy*, Judy Reiser discusses the extent to which belief in luck or in good and bad fortune has become central for many people.[4] In this provocative work, Reiser, a social worker, reports interviews with over six hundred people the majority of whom expressed strong beliefs in common superstitions, good luck charms, and a host of equally irrational ritual actions aimed at fending off evil and misfortune.

Personalized myths of fortune are reinforced by complementary cosmic myths that involve stories about generalized powers. These myths are presented in such movies as *Indiana Jones and the Temple of Doom* and stories about such things as the supposed curse of the long-dead Egyptian king Tutankhamen. The story of Tutankhamen is typical of how curse myths are generated. When the tomb was excavated in 1922, there was an unexpected delay in the opening of the burial chamber. An overzealous reporter wrote a story saying that this delay was due to the discovery of an "ancient Egyptian inscription" that laid a curse on anyone who entered the tomb. Five months later one of

---

[4]Reiser, *And I Thought I Was Crazy! Quirks, Idiosyncracies and Meshugass That People Are Into* (New York: Simon & Schuster, 1979).

the leaders of the expedition, Lord Carnarvon, died suddenly, and the story of the curse became firmly established in the public mind. In fact no such inscription had been found, and all the other members of the expedition, including those who were the first to enter the main chamber, lived long and successful lives.

A similar and highly popular myth of fortune is that of the so-called Bermuda Triangle, propagated in the mid-1970s. This myth is based on Charles Berlitz's book, which was on the New York best-seller list for twenty-six weeks in 1975 and has sold well over a million copies. Berlitz claims that a triangular area in the Carribean has long been the site of many mysterious events, such as the untraceable disappearance of aircraft and ships. In the wake of this book similar ones appeared, some elaborating the Bermuda Triangle story, others claiming to discover equally mysterious zones in different parts of the world. Once these "mysteries" were discovered, occult and bizarre solutions were proposed to "explain" them, ranging from alien spacecraft lying on the seabed to occult forces and cosmic rays. One author even suggested that the center of the Bermuda Triangle was the site of Hell and that it was the headquarters of the Devil on earth.

Actually the only mystery about the Bermuda Triangle is the phenomenal success of Berlitz's book and the positive reception it has received from a credulous public. But even this is not really mysterious. The truth of the matter is that the public prefers to assign cosmic importance to otherwise mundane fortune myths. To do so helps legitimize actions and beliefs that might otherwise be dismissed as neurotic.

Neopagan myths are centered on beliefs in earth spirits, plant intelligence, talking animals, hobbits, fairies, and other similar creatures. Lyall Watson's book *Supernature* provides a good example of the ways in which these myths are generated.[5] Writing in a pseudoscientific style and giving apparent "scientific evidence" for his nature mysticism, Watson creates an atmosphere in which belief in a magical world seems plausible.

The book begins with the statement "SCIENCE NO LONGER holds any absolute truth" and goes on to invoke an epistemological relativism that allows anything to seem to be true. The reasoning involved reminds us of the adage "When reason sleeps, monsters are born." Watson's world and that of believers in the new mythology quickly develop into a universe populated by sea

---

[5]Watson, *Supernature* (London: Hodder & Stoughton, 1974).

serpents, the Loch Ness monster, Bigfoot, and other creatures that supposedly hide from human beings. Fantastic as these tales may sound, many people believe in them—including anthropologist Carlos Castenada, whose books about Don Juan have an immediacy that is lacking in Watson's dry speculations. Invoking a magical world soon involves the believer in mystical powers, occult forces, and psychic radiations that are said to provide healing powers far in excess of the techniques of modern medicine.

Pseudoscience myths are stories about the nature and power of clairvoyance, E.S.P., and related phenomena. Books such as *The Geller Papers*, which is supposed to contain factual reports about the psychic abilities of Uri Geller, form the solid basis of these myths.[6] Geller, it will be remembered, is the modern "magician" who claimed to bend spoons and perform other feats through the power of his mind. Counterclaims by other competent magicians, such as James Randi, who has insisted that Geller has abused his skills as an entertainer, are conveniently overlooked by the press and gullible believers.

Another book promoting the mythologies of pseudoscience is Raymond A. Moody, Jr.'s *Life after Life*.[7] Moody interprets near-death experiences as phenomena confirming reincarnation and soul travel. Once again, his interpretations hold up only because they are not closely investigated. These and similar myths provide the basis for extravagant claims about the psychic powers of human beings. Professors Eysenck and Sargent, whose book *Explaining the Unexplained* is a partisan tract propagating belief in E.S.P. and related ideas, seem to lend further scientific respectability to all of these notions.[8]

Myths of technology are the final category of mythological fragments we should consider. These myths include stories about UFOs and lost worlds and civilizations. We call these "myths of technology" because they tell about beings who possess, or at some time in the distant past possessed, a technology far in advance of that of the modern world.

In their contemporary form, these myths seem to date from the publication of George Adamski and Leslie Desmons's best-selling book *Flying Saucers Have Landed*.[9] All later writings

[6]*The Geller Papers*, ed. Charles Penati (Boston: Houghton Mifflin, 1976).
[7]Moody, *Life after Life* (New York: Bantam Books, 1976).
[8]Hans J. Eysenck and Carl Sargent, *Explaining the Unexplained: Mysteries of the Paranormal* (London: Weidenfeld & Nicholson, 1982).

about flying saucers and alien visitors to earth draw heavily on this book for their central ideas. It should be noted that Adamski and Desmons, who told the world that they had actually entered an alien spacecraft, were themselves influenced by theosophical writings. Theosophically inspired thinking is found in other recent works, of which the most successful is probably Eric von Daniken's *Chariots of the Gods*.[10] However, John Michell's *The Flying Saucer Vision* (published a year before von Daniken's work) and Brad Steiger's *Gods of Aquarius* more clearly show the relationship between these tales and the new mythology.[11]

At a different level, but no less significant, are popular fantasy stories such as J. R. R. Tolkien's *The Lord of the Rings*, Poul Anderson's *The Broken Sword*, and Ursula LeGuin's *The Wizard of Earthsea*.[12] These stories create imaginative worlds in which the fantastic seems possible. Importantly, they do so very often in terms of pseudoscientific speculations about "alternate universes" and "space-time physics" that make the fantasies seem plausible.

As we discuss this complex series of myths, it is worth bearing in mind that most of these ideas were first introduced by science fiction writers. For example, L. Ron Hubbard experimented in his fiction with what was to become Scientology long before he created the organization. "Doc" E. E. Smith suggested that space visitors had influenced the history of the earth, and in his early space opera *Triplanetary*, he utilized the Atlantis myth and numerous other ideas popular in Theosophy and today's new religions.[13] It is little wonder that we see many flying saucer religions such as George King's Autherius Society, which was inspired by his book *You Are Responsible*, in which he claims to have "received" his religious message for our age from space "masters."[14]

---

[9]Adamski and Desmons, *Flying Saucers Have Landed* (London: T. Warner Laurie, 1953).

[10]Von Daniken, *Chariots of the Gods* (London: Souvenir Press, 1968).

[11]Michell, *The Flying Saucer Vision: The Holy Grail Restored* (London: Sphere Books, 1967); Steiger, *Gods of Aquarius* (New York: Harcourt Brace Jovanovich, 1976).

[12]Tolkien, *The Lord of the Rings* (London: Allen & Unwin, 1966); Anderson, *The Broken Sword* (New York: Ballantine, 1981); LeGuin, *The Wizard of Earthsea* (New York: Bantam, 1975).

[13]Smith, *Triplanetary* (1934; rpt., London: W. H. Allen, 1971).

[14]King, *You Are Responsible* (London: Artherius, 1961).

TOWARD A GENERAL MYTHOLOGY

So far we have simply identified various fragmented myths that are found in modern society. In the counterculture of the late 1960s, however, these unrelated fragments began to coalesce into more cohesive mythologies. They did not yet achieve the status of an officially sanctioned central mythology, but they did begin to make more sense than they had as isolated myths. The union of mythic fragments into a more general, self-reinforcing mythology involved three key sets of beliefs: decline beliefs, other civilization beliefs, and New Age beliefs.

Decline beliefs are elements of popular myths that reflect the pessimism of the counterculture concerning modern society. They are generalized stories about the decline of civilization and the end of the world. Essentially they hold that society as we know it is doomed. Ecological disaster and/or atomic war are thought to be imminent. Should we escape these, then a *1984*-style dictatorship awaits mankind. Doom or world catastrophe is an essential aspect not only of mythological structure but also of the structure of private visionary or conversion dreams. It is very much part of the mental map of the avant-garde hysteric, as we shall see.

The pessimism of decline beliefs is supported by stories and ideas ranging from those in such books as Hal Lindsey's *Late Great Planet Earth* to those in Howard Ruff's *How to Prosper during the Coming Bad Years* and Donella Meadows's *Limits to Growth*.[15] News reports, threats of financial instability, reports of wars and rumors of wars all feed the hunger for vicarious drama that is so central to the West's culture of hysteria. In the early 1970s, the Watergate scandal increased the plausibility of imminent doom. In the late 1970s, it was the oil crisis and inflation.

Vicarious doom provides those who participate in cultural hysteria with a new sense of mission. A new kind of citizen emerged in the form of survivalists. Their journals and specialist shops selling dehydrated foods grew as rapidly as did the mythology. Among the new religions, The Way was particularly influenced by the survivalist mentality. Members of The Way and even some members of the Mormon Church were advised to stockpile at least two years' supply of food in their basements.

---

[15]Lindsey, *The Late Great Planet Earth* (New York: Bantam Books, 1980); Ruff, *How to Prosper during the Coming Bad Years*, rev. ed. (New York: Warner Books, 1981); and Donella Meadows et al., *Limits to Growth: A Report for the Club of Rome's Project of the Predicament of Mankind* (New York: Universe Books, 1974).

As our imagination has reached forward into doom, so it has stretched backward into a glorious past and outward to embrace other planets. The second element of the emerging mythology consists of beliefs in other civilizations, usually civilizations greater than our own. The mythic significance of these ideas is that they form a theoretical bridge between the pessimism of decline beliefs and the optimism of New Age beliefs.

Other-civilization myths bring together a profound mistrust of modern science with a deep respect for science as mythology. Proponents of such myths speak about a golden age, which they project either into the past or onto an extraterrestrial civilization. The latter involves a vision of man's future. The former involves a nostalgic vision of the past that allows people to indulge vicariously in thoughts about prehistoric humans who lived in harmony with nature and possessed vast powers because they cooperated with natural forces to build great and enduring civilizations. Mythologizing science, myth merchants argue that hints of the powers of lost civilizations are found among Filipino psychic healers, South African bushmen, and other native peoples who retain some knowledge of nature spirits and forces. Why humans as a whole lost these wonderful powers and why those who possess them today live in abject poverty is never adequately explained. However, the fall of primal civilizations is typically explained in terms of pride and the misuse of magic.

Proponents of such myths maintain that the failure of orthodox archeologists to affirm this romanticization of civilizations simply proves how sterile modern science is and how much in need it is of the "creative" investigations of spiritual people. And so spiritualists conjure up visions of Atlantis, Mu, Lemurin, and other lost civilizations, embellishing them with complex comparisons and apparent erudition.

L. Sprague de Camp's book *Lost Continents* is important not only because he exposes the absurdity of these beliefs but because he relates these myths to nineteenth-century religious groups.[16] The *Book of Mormon* is based on the existence of a lost civilization built by North American Indians, and Theosophy appeals to stories about Atlantis. Other groups too invoke the idea of lost or extraterrestrial civilizations to objectify their claims. Hare Krishna believe in the Vedic civilizations of ancient India, while Jehovah's Witnesses have given evidence of a preoccupation with pyr-

---

[16]De Camp, *Lost Continents: The Atlantis Theme in History, Science and Literature* (New York: Dover Publications, 1970).

amids and sacred measurements. It would seem, in short, that myths of other civilizations perform an apologetic function by weaving observable "evidence," such as the Mayan ruins, into such a web of beliefs as to cloud the believer's doubts in its very complexity. And once the existence, or possibility of the existence, of these civilizations is accepted by the believer, belief in UFOs is confirmed.

Thus, both UFO sightings and other primal experiences receive "scientific" or "historical" confirmation from the general mythology. Without the mythology, many primal experiences would lack context and probably assume little significance in the life of an individual. But through the intervention of myth, primal experiences are seemingly confirmed by procedures that are deceptively like those of orthodox science. The result is a powerful belief system that is both self-confirming and self-authenticating. But the myths do not serve only to authenticate primal experiences; in a more important sense, they encourage people to have primal experiences in the first place, while at the same time amplifying their importance.

New Age beliefs are as optimistic as decline beliefs are pessimistic. And it is essentially the same mentality that conjures up doom that also conjures up bliss—and with the same degree of unreality. Both involve a vision of death followed by rebirth. Proponents of New Age beliefs hold that the night of doom will be followed by the dawn of the New Age of Aquarius.

Hippies of the sixties saw themselves as both the children of this new age and the heralders of its coming. Members of some of today's new religions believe that they are fulfilling the hippie vision. Writing about the advent of a new age, which she associates with what she terms "the Aquarian conspiracy," Marilyn Ferguson states that "the emergence of the Aquarian Conspiracy in the late twentieth century is rooted in the myths and metaphors, the prophecy and poetry of the past. Throughout history there were lone individuals here and there, or small bands at the fringes of science or religion who, based on their own experiences, believed that people might someday transcend narrow 'normal' consciousness and reverse the brutality and alienation of the human condition."[17]

The hope for this transformation is, according to Ferguson,

---

[17]Ferguson, *The Aquarian Conspiracy: Personal and Social Transformations in the 1980s* (Los Angeles: J. P. Tarcher, 1980), p. 45.

an "attack on the very foundations of Western thought." This attack, and the search for a new way of seeing, is the work of like-
minded people who, in the mid-seventies, formed the "conspiracy" that she is writing about. Normally conspiracy suggests
something sinister. But Ferguson intends it to mean a breathing
together of like-minded individuals in the spirit of the age, which
she contends is the Age of Aquarius, characterized by the "symbolic power of the pervasive dream in our popular culture: that
after a dark, violent age, the Piscean, we are entering a millennium of love and light—in the words of the popular song, 'The Age
of Aquarius,' the time of 'the mind's true liberation.'"[18]

Another popularizer of new myths, Lawrence Blair, has suggested that "the first burst of Aquarian enthusiasm experienced
by the young in the early 1960s has for many subsided into disen-
chanted apathy."[19] He goes on to argue, however, that the disen-
chantment is attributable to the fact that our cultures and individuals are experiencing a metamorphosis that will transform
mankind.

The sense of expectancy engendered by a strong belief in the
Age of Aquarius is often increased and sustained by talk about the
return of Christ. In such a context this orthodox Christian notion
is not used in its biblical sense to mean the return of Jesus and the
last judgment. Rather it has become a code expressing hope.

For some this hope is to be found in a new religious leader
who symbolizes the mission of Jesus and fulfills it in the creation
of an ideal world. Such an understanding of Christ's return is
found in the Unification Church, which equates the Reverend
Sun Myung Moon with Christ through a commonality of purpose.
For others, the return of Christ simply means the appearance of a
spiritual leader who is Christ-like. Still others talk of Christ's return in terms of a Christ spirit that will permeate the world. Certain fundamentalist biblical groups hold that Jesus will return
bodily and fulfill a number of specific prophecies. And various
other groups combine elements of all versions of Christ's return
in a confident but vague belief that things will someday get mirac-
ulously better.

In addition to beliefs about Christ, there are beliefs about
the coming of space lords and other aliens who will liberate man-

---

[18]Ferguson, *The Aquarian Conspiracy*, p. 19.
[19]Blair, *Rhythms of Vision: The Changing Patterns of Belief* (New York:
Schocken Books, 1976), p. 234.

kind and save us from the threat of atomic war. Once again, we should note that science fiction has played a key role in propagating and popularizing such views. Novels such as Arthur C. Clarke's *Childhood's End* and his more recent works suggest this theme in powerful ways.[20] While science fiction started the trend, science religions quickly developed and promoted beliefs in a variety of salvations brought about by benevolent space beings.

Other savior figures also feature in the myths of the new age. For many counterculture people in the late 1960s the mythic figure of Gandalf, the white wizard in Tolkien's *Lord of the Rings*, became a symbol of the new age. Others have developed beliefs about King Arthur and similar legendary heroes. We find "Buddhas" and "Krishnas" and such personalized saviors as the "Bhagwans." All are liberators sanctioned by one or another of these major coalescing myths.

Whoever the savior is to be and whatever the terms in which he or she is described, the mythic structure of beliefs surrounding the central figure is essentially the same. The savior is to come to change the world, to make it good and free from the terrors of modern life. Mankind will no longer be alone in a hostile universe but once more live in a personalized context in which human values will ultimately triumph.

The assurance of the final victory of good over evil comes from traditional legends, religious stories, and newly invented myths. But their authenticity within the mythology generally, and in new religions particularly, is always assured by the intervention of what Ferguson calls "human catalysts like the Aquarian Conspirators." More perceptively, we can speak of these agents as shamans or sorcerers who are initiators of change.

One such agent of consciousness is David Spangler of the Findhorn Community, who is described by many writers as one of the foremost leaders of the new age. In his book *Emergence: The Rebirth of the Sacred*, Spangler gives a coherent account of the new mythology as it is seen by an insider.[21] A similar and more elaborate development of the many aspects of the mythology discussed here can be found in Blair's *Rhythms of Vision*. Both of

---

[20]Clarke, *Childhood's End* (New York: Harcourt Brace Jovanovich, 1963).

[21]Spangler, *Emergence: The Rebirth of the Sacred* (New York: Delta Books, 1984). See also his *Revelation: The Birth of a New Age* (Middleton: Lorian Books, 1976).

these works, and many similar ones, not only articulate the coherence of the fragmented myths of modern society but bring them together in a pattern similar to the one we have outlined. Further, they add the final ingredient that provides these myths with the potential they need to become the central mythology of our society. It is to this question of the overall integration of the myths into a central framework that we now turn.

EVOLUTION AS CENTRAL MYTHOLOGY

In many ways the situation we face today in terms of our fragmented collection of disconnected myths is similar to that faced by the inhabitants of New England in the early part of the nineteenth century. Like us, the people of New England experienced rapid social change, including revolutions in transportation and communication. Their society was transient and uprooted. Traditional beliefs were on the wane and new ones vied for acceptance. In 1828 Thomas Dick wrote about the possibility of life on other planets in a book entitled *Philosophy of a Future State.* Swedenborgians speculated about spiritual "worlds." Ethan Smith pondered the origin of the American Indians in his book *A View of the Hebrews* (1825). People were fascinated with the Indian mounds that dotted the landscape. Stories about the pyramids of Egypt and lost civilizations were common.

Against this confused and confusing background, Joseph Smith, Jr., claimed to have discovered a book that explained the true facts about many of the puzzles that intrigued his contemporaries. In the *Book of Mormon* (1830), Smith laid the basis of a powerful mythology that wove together many diverse myths into an integrated whole. In his later "revelations," Smith elaborated these myths so that the developed mythology of Mormonism not only explained the origin of American Indians but also spoke about the significance of their archeological sites and speculated about life on other planets.

Fawn M. Brodie contends that Joseph Smith "was groping for a new metaphysics that would somehow take into account the new world of science. In his primitive and egocentric fashion he was trying to resolve the most troublesome philosophic problem of the nineteenth century."[22] Thomas O'Dea has argued that while

---

[22]Brodie, *No Man Knows My History,* 2d rev. ed (New York: Knopf, 1978), p. 172.

the *Book of Mormon* leaves much to be desired as literature, in its own terms and the context in which it was written, it was a challenging document "concerned fundamentally with the problem of good and evil."[23]

O'Dea cautions us against simply rejecting the *Book of Mormon* as an unbelievable and therefore unintelligible story. Rather, he maintains, it has an important intellectual element that gives its mythology an appeal far beyond the mere telling of tales. This element consists in the folksy but rational way in which Smith presents different viewpoints and argues for and against them.

An important element of Mormon mythology that gives it a continuing appeal is its use of evolutionary ideas. Smith wrote some thirty years before Darwin, but even at this earlier time evolutionary ideas were being hotly debated and widely disseminated in philosophical speculations. The influence of these ideas is especially evident in Smith's later work *The Book of Abraham* (1842) which, with the *Book of Mormon*, is regarded as divinely inspired scripture by Mormons.

Even more clear in its use of evolution as a mythological device is the book *Key to the Science of Theology* (1855), written by the Mormon apostle Parley P. Pratt.[24] Pratt speculates about mankind visiting other worlds in the future and places Mormon views of human life within the framework of spiritual evolution.

According to Mormon theology, human beings are spiritual beings whose existence predates their physical birth. They believe that our spirit bodies originated in eternity and that we progressed to earth to "gain a body" and undergo a probationary period that determines our future state. This spiritual evolution is covered by the "law of eternal progression." As their early leader Lorenzo Snow said, "As man is, God was; as God is man may become."[25] Evolution gives Mormon theology its essential unity.

Similar views about eternal progression and spiritual evolution are also found in other nineteenth-century new religions. Although different in her emphasis, Mary Baker Eddy, the founder

---

[23]O'Dea, *The Mormons* (Chicago: University of Chicago Press, 1964), p. 26.

[24]Pratt, *Key to the Science of Theology*, 10th ed. (Salt Lake City: Deseret Book, 1973), pp. 153-59.

[25]This well-known saying appears in many Mormon publications; see, for example, *Reflections on Mormonism*, ed. T. G. Madsen (Provo, Utah: Brigham Young University, 1978), p. 212.

of Christian Science, also used evolution to unify her creed. In the first edition of her fundamental work *Science and Health* (1875), she states quite clearly that "Mr. Darwin is right with regard to mortal man or matter, but he should have made a distinction between these and the immortal, whose basis is Spirit."[26]

Evolution was even more thoroughly adapted to religious needs by Helen P. Blavatsky, the founder of Theosophy. In her book *The Secret Doctrine* (1888), she speaks of moral development and individual lives in terms of cosmic evolution. Theosophy suggests that the inner, spiritual growth of mankind constitutes the heart and dynamics of the whole evolutionary process. Commenting on this, Bruce F. Campbell, a recent historian of Theosophy, says "a core of Theosophical teachings emerged. They are a synthesis of the idea of evolution with religious concepts chiefly from Hinduism and Buddhism."[27]

All of these movements and many others sought to integrate science, religion, and popular myth into an overall framework of evolutionary mythology that could fill the void left by the decline of traditional Christian views. But none of these attempts to create a new central mythology for society succeeded in capturing the imagination and commitment of most Westerners. In some ways German National Socialism and Italian Fascism proved more successful in meeting this goal. These ideologies also drew on the idea of evolution in such a way as to produce apparently powerful social mythologies.

This link between evolutionary belief as a mythology and fascism has long been recognized by historians of fascist movements. Joachim C. Fest, for example, has noted that "Hitler was influenced above all by the theories of the nineteenth-century social Darwinist school, whose conception of man as biological material was bound up with impulses towards a planned society." The effect of this on Hitler's actions is equally clear, as Fest points out: "Starting from the maxims of Struggle derived from social Darwinism, Hitler could see nothing in law or the institutions of justice but instruments for combating political foes."[28]

---

[26]See R. Peel, *Christian Science: Its Encounter with American Culture* (New York: Henry Holt, 1958), p. 91.

[27]Campbell, *Ancient Wisdom Revived: A History of the Theosophical Movement* (Berkeley and Los Angeles: University of California Press, 1980), p. 61.

[28]Fest, *The Face of the Third Reich: Portraits of the Nazi Leadership*, trans. Michael Bullock (New York: Pantheon, 1970), p. 212; cf. p. 28.

Reacting not only to the mythologization and politicization of evolution but more generally to the associated dangers of reductionism, Arthur Koestler has devoted considerable scholarly effort to questioning Darwinian evolution. Reductionism, he says, is "the philosophic belief that all human activities can be 'reduced' to i.e. explained by, the behavioural responses of lower animals . . . and that these responses in turn can be reduced to the physical laws which govern inanimate matter."[29] Koestler considers such reductionism to be dangerous because it leads to the denial of all values. "By its persistent denial of a place for values, meaning and purpose in the interplay of blind forces, the reductionist attitude has cast its shadow beyond the confines of science, affecting our whole culture and even political attitudes."[30] Once traditional moralities are declared obsolete on the basis of evolutionary development, the "higher" ideals of the party, whether fascist or communist, can be promoted regardless of human suffering and cost.

The devotion of fascists, communists, and other totalitarians to evolution as a central mythology explains why it is suspect in the political arena of the West. While it is not politically sanctioned, the myth of evolution nevertheless titillates the imagination. One could even argue that evolution has, in fact, attained the status of an official mythology in much of the public education of the West. It is taught not only in biology classes but as a heuristic framework in history and social studies.

C. S. Lewis expresses our attitude toward the mythologization of evolution when in his provocative essay "The Funeral of a Great Myth" he says, "we must sharply distinguish between Evolution as a biological theorem and popular Evolution or Developmentalism which is certainly a Myth. . . . In the science, Evolution is a theory about *changes:* in the Myth it is a fact about *improvements.*"[31]

We have already noted that nineteenth-century religious movements were developed and systematized by way of an evolutionary mythology. The evolutionistic framework has been similarly popular in the twentieth century, as for example in the writ-

[29]Koestler, *Janus: A Summing Up* (New York: London House, 1978), p. 19.

[30]Koestler, *Janus*, p. 25.

[31]Lewis, "The Funeral of a Great Myth," in *Christian Reflections*, ed. Walter Hooper (Grand Rapids: Eerdmans, 1971), pp. 83, 85.

ings of Roman Catholic scholar Pierre Teilhard de Chardin and British biologist Julian Huxley.[32] More importantly, it is a common theme in the literature of the new religious movements, as in Timothy Leary's seminal work *The Politics of Ecstasy*. Leary repeatedly links the use of LSD, spiritual evolution, the evolution of consciousness, and the development of new religions. He argues that the popular use of LSD heralds the next great evolutionary step for mankind. In his more recent work *Changing My Mind, among Others*, Leary develops evolution as a cultural myth by giving the reader a vision of a religious consciousness that will lead to the creation of a new humanity.[33]

Theodore Roszak's *Unfinished Animal: The Aquarian Frontier and Evolutionary Consciousness*,[34] Spangler's *Emergence*, and Blair's *Rhythms of Vision* are other general works that reflect "new age spirituality." All are structured by the mythological framework of evolution that binds together other fragmented myths and provides the basis for a new religious consciousness. Marilyn Ferguson speaks of evolution as "the new paradigm" and expresses faith that mankind is entering a new evolutionary phase during which we will control our evolutionary destinies. Not surprisingly, Ferguson finds in Arthur C. Clarke's *Childhood's End* an apt "literary metaphor" for what she claims "many serious scientists" actually believe is happening today.[35]

Evolution as myth can be distinguished from evolution as science by the type of question it tries to answer. Scientific evolution explains How; evolutionary myths explain Why. The mythology of evolution provides religious answers to ultimate human questions about meaning and purpose, while evolutionary science is simply meant to help us understand natural processes.

The success with which spiritual writers and pseudoscientists have advanced evolutionary myths reflects poorly on the educational system of Western society. With the development of modern education, the general public has come to *believe in* rath-

---

[32]See Teilhard de Chardin, *The Phenomenon of Man* (New York: Harper & Row, 1955); and Huxley, *Essays of a Humanist* (London: Chatto & Windus, 1965).

[33]Leary, *The Politics of Ecstasy* (London: Paladin, 1970); *Changing My Mind, among Others: Lifetime Writings* (Englewood Cliffs, N.J.: Prentice Hall, 1982).

[34]Roszak, *Unfinished Animal: The Aquarian Frontier and Evolutionary Consciousness* (London: Faber & Faber, 1975).

[35]Ferguson, *The Aquarian Conspiracy*, pp. 157-62.

er than *understand* modern science. Our culture is characterized more by a faith in science than by an appreciation of the scientific method and rational thought. What this means in essence is that we have allowed magic to replace science as knowledge and procedure.

In the literature of the new religions, faith in science has been transformed into a faith in a "new science," which is associated with an "emerging evolutionary consciousness." The shift in language reflects both a popular belief in science and a distrust of science as it is actually practiced by scientists. Modern science is distrusted because it has brought us the atomic bomb and ecological crises. But the faith in science remains. Instead of questioning the use of modern science or learning how science works, many people take the easy route of believing in the trouble-free faith of the new science.

The transition from belief in science to faith in a new science is most clearly made in Theodore Roszak's now classic work *The Making of a Counter-Culture*. Roszak attacks modern science because of its "objective consciousness" and control by experts. He then advocates the democratization of science by encouraging a return to a holistic vision based upon intuitive feelings, magic, and the way of the shaman.[36]

David Spangler merges popular mysticism and faith in science with new age beliefs in a similar fashion, using evolution to make shamanic conversations with nature spirits and disembodied intelligences appear reasonable.[37] William Irwin Thompson takes much the same approach, drawing on Freud's concept of the repressiveness of civilization:

> Now that the failure of the Green Revolution has dramatized the failure of the industrialization of agriculture, the underground traditions of animism can surface without any sense of embarrassment. . . . The iron winter of the industrial era is beginning its end. . . . Animism and electronics is the landscape of the New Age. . . . The people of Findhorn understand the place of technology in nature, and if they forget, the elves will soon let them know.[38]

[36]Roszak, *The Making of a Counter-Culture* (Garden City, N.Y.: Doubleday, 1969).

[37]Spangler, *Revelation: The Birth of a New Age* (Middleton: Lorian Press, 1983).

[38]Thompson, *The Findhorn Garden* (New York: Harper & Row, 1975), pp. ix-x.

The obvious flaw in this point of view is that the Green Revolution has not failed; to the contrary, it has saved millions of lives and greatly improved living standards throughout the world. Moreover, Thompson ignores the oppressiveness of animistic and magical beliefs and life in kin-based bands and tribes. Perhaps it is only the rich and leisured who can afford to glorify nature, spurn technological advances, and presume to commune with elves and other mythological creatures.

The new mythology is quite simply a return to magic. The Western world once evangelized the Third World. It would now seem that the Third World has in return shamanized the West. The proponents of many new religions are appealing to pseudoscience in their campaign to repudiate the real gains of modern technology and to embrace magic instead. Such a path has an obvious appeal: it offers quick and easy solutions, and it entails neither choice nor responsibility on our part. Maintaining a technological society, on the other hand, involves hard work, discipline, and education.

4

Modernity and the New
Mythology

The growing influence of the new mythology in even the most sophisticated populations in the West is a crucially significant development. It is not merely a reaction against what are widely perceived to be the limitations of science and reason. It is more significantly a reflection of essential human needs that have been met, and experiences that have been explained, throughout all ages and cultures in terms of religious, mythological, and/or magic-based idioms. As the technology of the modern world becomes more complex and incomprehensible, more people are seeking out religious, mythical, and magical frames of reference to make it palatable.

As we shall see later, the environment in which we live affects our inclination to adopt Christian, mythological, or magic-based idioms. Crises, guilt, and a deep sense of social injustice all influence members of modern societies as they have influenced people throughout human history. Environments characterized by such things as sharp economic fluctuations, physical dispossession, and social dislocation make people susceptible to dramatic mythological explanations of private and public conditions in the modern world as they have in the past.

In this chapter we will examine two areas of our lives—health and technology—that have recently been the focus of "modern" myth-making. Many people would be inclined to place the two together in a single category, on the assumption that both are closely related to modern science. But, as we will see, there is good reason to consider separately their incorporation into the new mythology and new religions.

HEALING MYTHS

Healing Myths are diverse stories about "spiritual," "holistic," and other alternative forms of healing. Some aspects of this mythological development are centrally important to those who join new religions.

It is very difficult to construct an objective analysis of the mythologies of healing. Many involve claims of miraculous healing, but the existence of spontaneous remissions and other natural healing processes makes such claims impossible to verify. These myths cover a vast range of beliefs, from traditional Christian ideas about prayer to the use of psychic powers and Scientology. In this discussion, we will restrict ourselves to a consideration of non-Christian beliefs, excluding the sorts of practices, as praying for the sick, that occur in all Christian churches. We will also differentiate myths of healing from genuine alternative medicines and traditional, nonmagical healing techniques. Herbal remedies, homeopathy, and similar methods of healing may not be accepted by many members of the medical profession, but they do have a rational basis and do not of necessity involve appeals to occult or mysterious powers even though they are often cited by magical healers in an attempt to legitimate fantastic claims.[1]

It is the mythological aspects of alternative healing as found in the "holistic health" and "human potential" movements and various new religions that interest us here.[2] The holistic health movement is a modern version of the magical health movement, and like various therapo-moral cults, which we will consider in a later chapter, it has roots in primal experiences. "Holistic health" is the modern expression of an ancient phenomenon. Its magical quality may not be immediately obvious because it tends to be cloaked in evolutionary and pseudoscientific language.

---

[1]Brian Inglis has written two books that deal with alternative medicine in a helpful and reasonable fashion: *Fringe Medicine* (London: Faber & Faber, 1964) and *Natural Medicine* (Glasgow: Collins, 1979). Inglis provides a scholarly account of alternative medicines without appealing to or elaborating on their possible mythic significance.

[2]Paul C. Reisser, Teri K. Reisser, and John Weldon offer a valuable Christian critique of the magical holistic health movements in their book *The Holistic Healers* (Downers Grove, Ill.: InterVarsity Press, 1983).

There are obvious links between the modern movement and nineteenth-century religious movements. Almost without exception the creeds of major new religions of the past century contained a strong healing element. The magical aspects of Mormonism were expressed in *The Word of Wisdom,* which prohibits the drinking of tea and coffee and advocates various other health laws. It is also present in the Mormon practice of the laying on of hands and in their belief that their priesthood can effect spiritual healings. Christian Science upholds the health beliefs of Mary Baker Eddy's theology, and Christian Science practitioners conduct healing services. Seventh-Day Adventists, Theosophists, and even Jehovah's Witnesses, with their prohibition of blood transfusions, all exemplify the drive to combine religion and spiritual healing under the umbrella of magic.

Because of their seemingly greater affinity to science, the most important "healing" phenomena are the mythological elaborations of the new psychotherapies. This magico-moral cult activity has given expression to myriads of new therapies that have turned the West, as Martin L. Gross has suggested, into a "psychological society."[3] Psychological healing myths have generated a systematic and identifiable social structure consisting of new messiahs, new therapies, and citizen-patients.

New therapies include primal scream and its messiah Arthur Janov, feeling therapy and its messiah Joseph Hart, reality therapy and its messiah William Glasser, gestalt therapy and its messiah Fritz Perls, and Group Dynamics and its messiah Daniel Casriel. Eric Berne and Thomas A. Harris popularized Transactional Analysis (TA), Alexander Lowen started Bio-Energetic Analysis, Ida Rolf invented Rolfing, and Paul Bindrim introduced Nude Marathon Regression Therapy. There is also the somewhat older Logotherapy of V. E. Frankl and the *Daseinanalyse* of Ludwig Binswanger. All of these form part of what is now called the "human potential" or "human growth" movement and are sanctioned by the scientific community as humanistic psychology. Among the giants in this mythological framework of humanistic psychology are Carl Rogers, who originated client-centered therapy; Alan Watts, the East-West philosopher who developed the expanded-consciousness movement; Bill Schutz, who became the "Messiah of Joy"; Fred Stoller, who popularized Marathons; and Abraham Maslow, who introduced "peak experiences" into the popular idiom.

---

[3]Gross, *The Psychological Society* (New York: Random House, 1978).

All these manifestations of the human potential movement stress personal growth, happiness through encounter, the here and now, the body and body techniques, emotion, feeling, peak experiences, or bottomless pain. As in non-Western, pre-industrial societies, emphasis is placed on touching, massaging, hugging, palpitating, and vibrating the body to elicit feeling. Awareness is in; blocking, especially intellectual blocking, is out.

In the Third World, all these body-based shamanic techniques are used to treat physical ailments and psychological problems that have become somatic. In the West the emphasis is on encouraging the body to eliminate, ejaculate, vibrate, palpitate, and so on in order to increase awareness and to carry the human spirit closer to its goal of ultimate spiritual liberation. To reach the beyond of our ultramodern imagination, we are told to return to ancient techniques of gyrating the body.

It is very significant that most members of new religions (especially Rajneeshies) have participated in more than one—and sometimes more than a dozen—different kinds of these therapies and practices. While psychotherapy groups, new left political communes, and new religions appear to be separate organizational entities, a common thread runs through them. We find, for example, that an individual who has joined one of them will very often have sampled indiscriminately among the others as well. On further investigation, we find that members of new religions often share three significant characteristics. First, they tend to make a relatively poor start in life (e.g., being expelled from school) and they generally have some form of personality disorder. Second, after indulging in a "career" of communal life, participation in different psychotherapy and other "fringe" groups, such as caravans, the theater, and radical political organizations, they will typically describe themselves as paranoid, alienated, experiencing a state of mental crisis, having a nervous breakdown, feeling hopeless or immobile, and shaken by bouts of crying. Third, following this period of heightened emotional and mental chaos, many settle for one new religious movement and are content to remain with it for a number of years.

The following are two examples of such "careers" into the world of the new mythology.

The first individual, a young man, received counseling at school without any apparent success, for he was expelled. During the next few years he associated with people who were using LSD. He joined a hippie commune and from there moved into other drug-based communes. Then he met Douglas Harding and practiced his and Baba Ram Dass's consciousness raising and self-actualization. Following this experience, he joined a Tibetan monastery, moved into a Harding commune, and joined a theater group. None of these experiences gave him peace or a sense of self-control. He described himself as "paranoid" and "alienated" and spoke of having suffered a "nervous breakdown" that left him "immobile" and continuously crying. Emerging from this bout of cultural hysteria, he joined a Rajneesh Center, where he engaged in dynamic meditation, screaming therapy, and sexual therapy. Having sent his body through these gyrations, he set off for Poona, India (at that time the Rajneesh headquarters), where he participated in "lots" of group encounter therapies.

The second individual had a similar career into and out of cultural hysteria by way of emotion-cum-body pummeling. He was an adopted child whose parents divorced before he was ten years old. He witnessed his mother's nervous breakdown and was subsequently expelled from school. At the age of thirteen he was deeply into Buddhism and Zen Buddhism. When he was seventeen he traveled to India. In Pakistan he joined a Sufi community. He returned to England and lived in a religious caravan that he called "the Littlest Monastery of the Way." Then he joined a Zen Buddhist monastery. He left this to follow a Tibetan master. Then he entered psychodrama therapy and participated in Jerzy Grotowski's drama teachings. Later he himself became a practitioner of drama therapy. He also practiced bioenergetics, hypnotherapy, and Gestalt therapy. He went on to learn dynamic meditation with Rajneeshies in Devon. He participated in rebirthing therapy, and then joined a progressive/political growth community. After all this, he described himself as being in a state of "crisis." He said he "felt helpless," entered an "immobile" period, and, emerging from this, returned to Devon. Dissatisfied still, he left for Poona again. Here he says he had a "fantasy" about "drastic change" and about the possibility that he "might even disappear." Thereafter he remained a Rajneeshie.

TECHNOLOGICAL INNOVATION AND THE MYTH OF MODERNITY

If new religious movements simply consisted of a creative interaction between mythology, primal experiences, and aspects of the great religious traditions, they would be interesting but not particularly new. Throughout history, religious movements have

arisen through a recombination of existing ideas and experiences. Today's new religions are new in the sense that they develop differently than these historic religions. Specifically, their nov-
elty consists in the ways they incorporate modern technology and
cross-cultural knowledge. High technology has not only been
mythologized but has fundamentally changed our attitudes toward the past, present, and future.

Defining *modernity* is difficult. In the common parlance it is
usually associated with what is up-to-date, with trendy fashions,
with an attitude of commitment to the future in its full connota-
tive sense of looking outward in time and space rather than backward to the past. Roger Scruton has suggested that *modernity* sig-
nifies "the transformed consciousness of the word and the self
that comes from living *now* rather than *then*."[4] A preference for
things of the future rather than things of the past is essential to the
concept of modernity. Modernists place more value on the advancement of industry, science, and technology than on their history generally, and on religious authority specifically.

Some have interpreted the counterculture phenomenon of
the sixties as a romantic revolt against science and modernity, but
in fact it was not. At most, it was a revolt against the grip that *Western history*—the past—has had on our society's methods of pro-
duction and institutions. Today, groups continue to express concern about technological progress, capitalism, and specific issues
(e.g., genetic engineering), but the vast majority seem to be enjoying a quiet honeymoon with high technology. This points to the
fact that the meaning of the term *modern* is by no means simple.
Technology makes use of old traditions along with the new. The
important thing to remember is that these old traditions have
been *dislocated* in time and space. What has really been done
away with is a sense of history; it has been replaced by a form of
eclecticism.

VENERATION OF THE PAST

This inclination to accept modernity and science and their religious implications is relatively new. In fact most religious people,
including prominent theologians, have done little in the way of
assessing the intellectual and social significance of modernity.
The majority of religious scholars still view history as a process of

---

[4]Scruton, *A Dictionary of Political Thought* (London: Pan Books, 1983),
pp. 302-3.

unbroken development from the time of Jesus to the present. Such an attitude fundamentally distorts their understanding of our time and prevents their fully appreciating the significance of new religious movements.

As we have noted, the idea of enlightenment and the sense of a radical break with past history are key to the notion of modernity. The sense of a break with the past is very evident in the contrast between today's popular attitudes toward the "here and now" and those of former generations. Until the last two decades of the eighteenth century, most people in our culture viewed the past with a sense of loss. European schools taught the works of classical Greek and Roman authors, and only the most optimistic educators dared to hope that their generation might attain the heights of achievement of classical civilization. Scarcely any thought was given to the possibility of surpassing the ancients. Every educated person took it as a matter of course that the glory of European civilization—and all other great civilizations, for that matter—lay in the past.

In the premodern world, ancient things and ideas were respected and revered. Change, such as it was, came slowly, and was largely restricted to such characteristically ephemeral things as fashions in clothing. Like Solomon, premodern sages could assert confidently that there was nothing new under the sun. It was assumed that a fortunate person might see everything anyone could possibly hope to see in the course of a lifetime.

Veneration of the past was a social reality because technological change was painfully slow, and educated men from the fifth to the end of the eighteenth century were aware that Roman civilization was more advanced than anything they might achieve. It was assumed that the Romans and their predecessors, the Greeks and Egyptians, had realized the essence of civilization and had developed their technology to unsurpassed heights. Indeed, many Roman technological feats were not repeated for hundreds of years because the art of manufacturing such things as concrete had been lost with the collapse of the Western empire.

THE IMPINGEMENT OF MODERNITY ON LIFE

A history of technological change shows relatively little innovation in the period from Roman times to the eighteenth century. Of course such change was not entirely absent—the invention of the modern printing press in the middle of the fifteenth century, for instance, altered many aspects of society. But such changes were the exception, not the rule. In many areas of life technological skills actually deteriorated from the heights attained in Roman times.

It was not until the latter part of the eighteenth century that real technological progress began to occur. With the discovery of various metalworking techniques, it became possible to manufacture steam engines and put them to use. It is the speed of this translation of discovery and invention into use that is remarkable. For example, within one year of its invention, the steam engine was used to power boats; within three years, it was used to spin cotton; within forty years it was used to power railroad locomotives.

The expansion of the railways in the nineteenth century, more than anything else, changed the social composition of countries and the outlook of peoples. Travel was no longer a privilege of the few, nor was it dangerous or uncomfortable. A whole new way of seeing the world had been created. For the first time since the Roman legions withdrew from Britain in A.D. 410, it was possible not only to travel from London to Rome safely but to travel faster than had ever been possible before. The realization grew that in one respect anyway, the once-vaunted Romans had been surpassed by a succeeding generation.

The effect of many such apparently simple changes were far reaching, if little appreciated. A new outlook on life emerged. Instead of looking to the past for guidance and direction, people began to look to the future. It is not surprising that the futuristic works of Jules Verne (1828-1905) and others like him should have become popular at this time. And for the first time, scientists became folk heroes. The entire basis of daily life changed as agricultural societies were transformed into urban industrial societies.

IMPLICATIONS OF TECHNOLOGICAL CHANGE
FOR CHRISTIANITY

The change of attitude toward the past and the future was paralleled by a profound but little recognized change of attitude toward religion in general and Christianity in particular. Prior to the nineteenth century, Christians identified with the wisdom of the ages and claimed the heritage of Roman civilization. Christians were able to argue that the Romans were the most advanced people on earth and that at the height of their achievements they had chosen Christianity. If Christianity was good enough for the advanced and sophisticated Romans, it should surely be adequate for less advanced and more barbaric peoples.

Miracles, prophecy, and a host of other beliefs that modern people find problematic were not an issue for our ancestors. Indeed, Christian apologists freely appealed to miracles and prophecy as evidence for the truth of Christianity. In the period from the fall of Rome to the nineteenth century, very few people questioned the essential claims of the church. Such skeptics as did make their presence felt were generally considered misfits who were objecting to the whole trend of European civilization. If the Romans could accept the validity of miracles, then how could less-educated people with a lower level of scientific and technological skill possibly doubt them?

All of this changed in the nineteenth century. The intellectual doubts of a few individuals in the eighteenth century became a torrent of skepticism as ordinary people experienced the impact of technological change in their daily lives.

Suddenly progress made the Greeks and the Romans appear ignorant and pre-scientific. We became more aware of their superstitions and irrationality. The conversion of Roman civilization to Christianity was no longer considered remarkable; it simply confirmed the credulity of ignorant people. Religion was, in other words, old fashioned. For the first time since the conversion of the Roman empire, Christians found themselves on the defensive against progress and the findings of science. Miracles and prophecies that had once been convincing now became embarrassments. It was as if science had declared biblical reality a primitive illusion.

The rapidity with which Christianity lost its dominant position as the preserver of civilization and knowledge in the West has not been fully appreciated by most people. Indeed, one might say the church is still in a state of culture shock following its loss of respect and authority. Nevertheless, there is no disputing the fact that the church is no longer at the center of our culture. It has been replaced by the sciences. Among other things, this displacement has created a spiritual vacuum—and it is now being filled by new religions.

In the nineteenth century, such thinkers as Auguste Comte, T. H. Huxley, and Karl Marx felt that science could replace religion as the universal source of meaning for humans. As the twentieth century dawned, however, the limitations of science became clear. While it excelled in answering questions about the

How of things, it had no answers concerning their Why. Instead of providing new meaning, it accelerated the loss of faith. Ultimate questions remained unasked and unanswered. In the long run, people find such a situation unbearable, especially when primal experiences, joys, and tragedies shake their complacency. In such a context, religion finds a ready response—and new religions, which speak the idiom of modernity, thrive.

In the past, when a people's confidence in modernity and a purely secular existence was shaken, it was expected that they would turn to traditional Christianity. Such an expectation is no longer valid. It underestimates the appeal of modernity. People are not much inclined to turn to the church, because from childhood they have been taught that Christianity is old fashioned, that it has been disproved. Many people suppose that Christianity conflicts with the findings of science and that it must therefore be wrong. Predictably, many youths are more inclined to turn to new religions or new forms of old religions, which are not tainted by the charge of being old fashioned.

Some reactionary new religions reject scientific aspects of modernity without rejecting its technology. They deny scientific findings on the grounds that such findings contradict the "true Christianity" that they claim to represent. Converts to these new religions rarely realize that they are not really embracing historical Christianity. Historical Christianity has not rejected science. The gurus of these new religions claim continuity with the Christian tradition, but in fact they are like the gurus of other new religions that are not even nominally Christian because they have no ties to any historical past. They have rejected history and reason, and in doing so they have rejected the God of historical Christianity as well.

MORMONISM: A NEW RELIGION BASED ON A NEW MYTHOLOGY

Mormonism, or the Church of Jesus Christ of Latter-Day Saints, is one of the first religious movements to display clearly the influence of modernity. Founded in 1830 with the publication of the *Book of Mormon*, this new religion is an intriguing blend of old and new. The *Book of Mormon* itself is a form of "Christian" romance. It tells the story of two groups of Jews who left Jerusalem and eventually settled in the Americas. Their descendants then experienced periods of revival and apostasy until finally Jesus preached the gospel to them following his resurrection. Finally, however, the apostates massacred the true believers and degenerated into a state of barbarism.

As a romantic novel, the *Book of Mormon* is basically Christian. With the exception of its teaching about the Fall, its theology is simple and fundamentally orthodox. It does, however, embellish the biblical account when it clarifies certain points that are seemingly unclear in the Bible (e.g., the proper mode of baptism). Nevertheless, its overall orthodoxy is used to great advantage by Mormon missionaries in presentations to unsuspecting people who come from Christian backgrounds. It is of course more difficult to convince the potential convert of the "historical" truth of the book in light of its rather unusual and farfetched story about the migration of Jewish peoples to the Americas. On the whole, however, Mormons encounter fewer objections concerning doctrinal deviations than do disciples of other new religions.

The effects of modernity on Mormonism are best seen in the later "revelations" of Joseph Smith and the "scriptures" he claimed to have discovered. A prime example is *The Book of Abraham*, which is found in the Mormon *Pearl of Great Price*. These works develop the theme of eternal progression—the doctrine that human souls exist prior to their earthly lives. This doctrine, which is the cornerstone of modern Mormon theology, is clearly a mythologization of the idea of progress and evolutionary philosophy.

The genius of Smith was his ability to appeal to the common man, to people with little to no education. He took progressive and fashionable ideas, embedded them in specific contexts of "new revelations," and told these in the form of stories resembling those of the biblical writers. As Fawn Brodie shows in her brilliant biography of Joseph Smith, he was a popularizer of new ideas.[5] More importantly, he was able to turn the confusion produced by intellectual and social change into new certainty, and he did so by being sensitive to the idiom of his audience. In Mormonism, modernity finds its first great religious expression, although it is combined with ideas from the Abramic tradition.

During the nineteenth century, there emerged other religious movements that responded in equally creative ways to modernity. Most of these movements were short-lived. Others, such as Christian Science, are still with us.

---

[5]Brodie, *No Man Knows My History* (New York: Knopf, 1963).

THE MYTH OF MODERNITY: A SUMMATION

In the final analysis, the myth of modernity consists of an acceptance of high technology and continued responsible technological progress. Its gurus reject the notion that everything can be explained solely in terms of reason and intellect. Both gurus and their followers have tired of professional explanations of private, social, or political conditions. Modern mythologizers rarely idealize our historical past, although sometimes they project an imagined "golden tradition" into the future. On the other hand, most members of new religions romanticize the remnants of the traditional—especially the non-Western traditional world. Modern romanticism and pastoralism together constitute the modern mythological idiom, a way of thinking centered not on our historical past but rather on other cultures.

Many of today's youths are particularly susceptible to the new mythological idiom because, at its best, it is at once very up-to-date, cross-cultural, experiential, and deeply spiritual in nature. In this sense, new religions constitute an expression of revolt, much as sects once did, against the unquestioned central authority not only of orthodox Christianity but also of a life explained and ordered by specialists and dominated by the intellect.

Among the disadvantages of this loyalty to the new mythological idiom is the fact that just as the religious emphasis is currently no longer on suffering but on health, positive energy, euphoria, and peak experiences, so the mythological emphasis is no longer on a painstaking adherence to scientific method but on its fruits—namely, high technology and the comfortable lifestyles it can afford. This attitude is dangerous, for no tree can bear fruit without nourishment from its roots. Our society will not be able to enjoy the fruits of the work of past generations for long if it does not make contributions of its own.

CONCLUSION

The new mythology is opposed to science as method and knowledge, yet it hungrily accepts its products, almost to the point of gluttony. While those who have accepted the new mythology do not venerate our past, they are curiously intoxicated with the traditions of non-Western societies. It is in this sense that the new mythology can be said to produce modern versions of romanticism and pastoralism. Despite their nominal celebration of democratic ideals, the new myth-makers have embarked upon a reactionary adventure with the aim of reestablishing a hierarchical world based on the power of privilege and wealth unrestrained by reason. They are willing to discard democratic traditions that have served Western culture for millennia in favor of a mystical revival reminiscent of the thirteenth-century revival that put an end to the great advances made during a twelfth-century renaissance. Instead of bringing light, the new mythology is ushering in a new dark age, complete with a priesthood of occult authorities who control power and limit knowledge.

In subsequent chapters we will investigate the neoconservatism of most new religions. It is the irony of our age that phenomena called futuristic are in fact conservative and even reactionary. As fragments of many diverse myths have combined into a general mythology of modernity and healing myths in our culture, they have followed this same conservative impulse. What the new mythmakers and the disciples of some new religions have heralded as a step into a new age is in fact a retreat into the bitter past gilded by tales of imaginary old or non-Western civilizations. The highs from LSD, meditation, trance, or the touch of a "spiritual master" that the new religions present as the means by which we can be catapulted into a new age and a new transcendent consciousness are in fact just different versions of techniques and talismans used by ancient shamans and diviners—the sorts of things we once dismissed as "primitive" and "constricting." The new religionists and new mythmakers would have us believe that ancient practices that once served as desperate defenses against a narrow existence filled with monotonous routines are now a key to the future. Serious anthropological work has demonstrated how stressful the old "commune" life was, with its suspicions, jealousies, and above all its unrelenting pressures to conform, but all of that is ignored by popularizers who feel the need to romanticize the past.

While the contents of myths vary, their structures are remarkably uniform. Both public myth and private conversion dream have the same form. A vision of world catastrophe is followed by death and rebirth. These are given cosmic importance, and the mythmaker or dreamer becomes imbued with a sense of mission. Conversion and commitment, though private and mundane, are projected onto the world as an evolutionary process. Indeed, as we will see later, the conversion process, once but a feature of adolescent development, has in our free society been extended into adulthood. We are now willing to entertain alternate ways of life and reach for imaginary higher levels of evolution throughout our lives.

And so we note, not without some shock, the limitations of human imagination. Mythical structures, like the structures of dreams and fantasies, would appear to be as fixed as the instinctual behavior patterns of animals on the lower rungs of the evolutionary ladder. Fantasies, dreams, myths, and science fiction stories are filled with colorful content, an eclectic carousel of uniforms, sensualized high technology, lurid vapors, and ancient rituals that are sometimes violent, often pornographic, and always primitive, repressive, and deadening of reason and the critical sense. The new mythmakers would have us believe that this content is ultramodern, but it is quite the opposite. It is not possible to break through to modernity without the rigorous exercise of rational thought. The melodramatic fantasies that are so prominent a feature on the screens and in the novels of our culture only serve to jade our senses and numb our minds.

5

The Primal Core

At the heart of many religious movements, particularly new religions, lie "primal experiences"—unexpected vivid encounters that are considered to be other than "normal." Such experiences take many forms. Above all, they not only shock those who experience them but also bring about a change in their attitude toward the material world. Primal experiences involve such things as dreams, visions, voices, spiritual healings, a sense of presence, notions of destiny, sightings of ghosts, inexplicable spiritual phenomena, and other "occult" events.

Primal experiences are important for new religious movements because they affirm the reality of the new mythology. Before a person has a primal experience, he or she may view the new mythology as simply an unusual or even intriguing way of seeing the world. But following such an experience, even novel myths seem unremarkable and acceptable.

Primal experiences give life to mythology in a startling way. They are enough out of the ordinary that secular society tends to deny that they are real. And because primal experiences are unusual, medical and psychiatric establishments identify them as abnormal and classify the people who have them as disturbed or mentally ill. Naturally, most people do not welcome being labeled in this fashion, and so even people whose lives are changed by primal experiences are often reluctant to talk about them.

Nevertheless, many people do speak of having primal experiences outside the context of a new religion. When they later join a movement of their choice, they note that in the outside world they had felt odd and uneasy about telling anyone of their experience but that within the new religion they have found a ready audience. They find that other members of the new religion not only take their particular experience seriously but reinforce its reality by relating tales about similar experiences that others have had. More importantly, new converts find that within the new religion their hitherto unexplained and somewhat embarrassing experiences are given a convincing theological interpretation in terms of the ideology of the group.

A sense of divine guidance or destiny is fostered, and individuals are persuaded that their experiences constitute a call to join the group. Dreams and visions confirm the rightness of this calling, as do group discussions, lectures, and "sharing sessions." Within the context of these intimate meetings, potential recruits and established members talk freely about primal experiences, and members testify to the reality of the spirit world in their lives.

As it turns out, primal experiences are remarkably common. Professor David Hay became interested in the phenomenon when some postgraduate students at the University of Nottingham, England, responding to a survey admitted that they had had primal experiences that profoundly affected their outlook.[1] The majority of these students said that they had no adequate explanation for their experience and would welcome one. Following this initial survey, Professor Hay and Professor Ann Morisy arranged a statistically valid national survey of the British population. In this more qualified survey they found that 36.4 percent of those included in the random sample reported having had such experiences. Significantly, 45 percent of those who had had these experiences had had no real contact with churches or organized religions.[2]

In a national survey in the United States, some 30 percent of Americans responded positively to questions about primal experiences. A much higher figure was obtained by Robert Wuthnow in his survey of the San Francisco Bay area population. There

---

[1]See Hay, "Reports of Religious Experiences by a Group of Postgraduate Students: A Pilot Study" and "Religious Experiences among a Group of Postgraduate Students: A Qualitative Survey," unpublished papers presented at the Colloquium on Psychology and Religion, Lancaster University, 1975.

[2]Hay and Morisy, "Reports of Ecstatic Paranormal or Religious Experiences in Great Britain and the United States: A Comparison of Trends," *Journal for the Scientific Study of Religion*, 1/7: 255-65.

Wuthnow's positive response rate went up to 50 percent.[3] In Canada, Reginald Bibby found that 60 percent of Canadians reported positively when asked about primal experiences. All of this evidence suggests, Bibby observed, a "pool of religiosity" that is largely untapped by established religions.[4]

Similar findings are reported from the Third World and other industrial nations. In his studies of hundreds of Zulu in South Africa, for example, S. G. Lee reports that before individuals would become diviners in divining cults, they would have a variety of primal experiences, including numerous visual and auditory hallucinations. Fifteen percent reported a history of minor possession that involved fugue states, hallucinations, dreaming, and so on. Seventeen percent reported diseases that they attributed to sorcery. The difference between those who merely consulted diviners and those who actually became diviners was largely a matter of the severity of their condition. Chronic or severe sufferers went through rigorous, six-month-long initiations, and converted from client to diviner to have their "ways cleared."[5]

CASE HISTORIES

In order to give an indication of both the wide range of differences in the life histories of members of new religions and the important similarities among them, we present four case histories, using the mythical "New Dispensation Church" as a representative new religion. The reader should note the significant role that primal experiences and fragments of the new mythology play in the lives of all four individuals either before they join their new religion (as is most often the case) or after they join it.

Our studies are not unique.[6] We present them because most authors who document the occurrence of similar primal experi-

---

[3]Wuthnow, *Experimentation in American Religion: The New Mysticisms and Their Implications for the Churches* (Berkeley and Los Angeles: University of California Press, 1978), p. 100; cf. pp. 64-65.

[4]Bibby, "Religionless Christianity: A Profile of Religion in the Canadian '80s," *Social Indicators Research* 13 (1983): 1-16. See also Stark and Bainbridge, *The Future of Religion: Secularization, Revival and Cult Formation* (Berkeley and Los Angeles: University of California Press, 1985), pp. 325ff. And see Hardy, *The Spiritual Nature of Man* (Oxford: Clarendon Press, 1979).

[5]Lee, "Spirit Possession among the Zulu," in *Spirit Mediumship and Society in Africa*, ed. J. Beattie and J. Middleton (New York: Africana, 1969), pp. 128-55.

[6]For similar case studies, see Beckford, *Cult Controversies: The Societal Response to the New Religious Movements* (London: Tavistock Publications, 1985), and Barker, *The Making of a Moonie* (Oxford: Basil Blackwell, 1985).

ences fail to recognize the fact that interviewees interpret them as evidence of the reality of the new mythology. It is this power of primal experiences to transform extraordinary mythology into ordinary reality that helps propel potential converts into a group of their choice.

Raymond: Spiritual Seeker

Raymond was born into poverty in 1953 in Central Canada. He had a family, including two brothers, but he cannot remember them. By the time he was two years old, he was in a foster home. His memory starts there, in that Pentecostal foster home, with the regular beatings he received from the family's adolescent son.

Once he was beaten into unconsciousness, an event he remembers to this day as the occasion on which he developed a deep and abiding resentment. It was then, when he was about five years old, that he concocted a scheme to kill the son of his foster parents by placing razor blades in his bed. He was saved from this act of revenge when his mother kidnapped him. What he did not escape, however, was poverty, for he remembers that his mother took him to a dump to find blankets for him.

The stay with his mother was brief—a few months, maybe a year. All he remembers is that she was very religious and taught him to pray. He began to believe in something.

He was soon taken to a new foster home and found it to be worse than the first. He fought frequently, at the same time fearing the evil within him that made him fight. And when they chained him to a doghouse and fed him dog food for days at a time, he began to feel it was right. Chained, he felt at peace, as if the chain restrained his otherwise unchecked self-hate.

He remembers running away somehow and living among Cree Indians for a few months. He remembers being among animals and feeling befriended by them. He remembers talking to them and feeling less lonely among them. And he remembers learning about Manitou, the Indian conception of God. His association with Cree Indians heightened his suggestibility.

When he was seven, he was back with his real family. His appendix was removed. During the operation, he remembers quite clearly a feeling that he was outside of his body.

By age eight he was in another foster home. One event from this period stays in his memory: he ate a full jar of honey, became sick, and was in a coma for a week. During that coma, he entered a loving world that would be his alone for many years to come. He calls it the spirit world. It was filled with "friends" that would visit him in recurrent dreams and in his subsequent retreats to it.

At age nine he was back with his family. Hate, isolation, and tension formed the essence of family life. It also gave rise to his first stomach ulcer.

So difficult was his reality that he learned to visit the spirit world regularly. He was, in fact, preoccupied with it. He would sit on his bed, visualize the spirit world, fashion it to his liking, and enter it. Once inside, he would be reunited with his former friends.

His spiritual preoccupations became obvious. When he was ten, his brother discovered him talking to his invisible friends. The brother alerted his parents, who must have listened in, for he was taken first to a psychiatrist and then to an exorcist. They resented the expense of these visits.

He became an altar boy in the Catholic Church, but he found no solace. Shortly before his eleventh birthday, he decided to end his life. It was his intention to commit suicide on the day of his birth. The day arrived. He was on his way to throw himself in front of a bus at a chosen street corner when he was struck by a question. The thought flashed through his mind: "What if I am the returned Christ?" He had heard a fair amount about the second coming of Christ just previously, and he was captivated by the idea. He forgot suicide. Christ was suffering, and he was Christ. He came to believe he had been Christ for two years, a period, he remembers, that had been filled with questions to God. He asked, and God answered through his inner voice. "And the answers," he added, "resembled the teachings of the New Dispensation Church."

He had never told his mother that he believed himself to be Christ. But once, when he was thirteen and she was beating him for something, she said "And you are not the returned Christ." That was it. He began to question who Christ really was. He read the Bible and asked priests, but their answers seemed hollow, and he felt that they were accusing him of dabbling with Satan. Disillusioned, he gave up attending the Catholic Church.

Seeing himself as somehow chosen, and filled with a sense of moral injustice in the world, he joined the Socialist Student League. To his mind, Christ was a socialist. And socialists shared. This fit in with his deep bitterness and resentment toward the rich. He started taking LSD and then marijuana and then hashish. He also studied the martial arts.

During this phase he shifted between retreats into his spirit world and increasingly open displays of violence. Christ and God were dead. He was a socialist and he felt embittered toward the rich. At age sixteen, he mobilized over six hundred students from three schools. The brief moment of glory was soon over, though, because he dealt in drugs, was in frequent trouble with the police, and was quickly abandoned by his socialist friends.

His violence increased, and he looked for a philosophy that would accommodate it. He found it in Kung Fu and the martial arts, at which he was now adept. By the time he was twenty, his spiritual development had halted, but his violence was increasing. He resented the Catholic Church, scorned priestly celibacy, lived with one girl after another, dealt with drugs, and participated in the underworld. As he grew older, the condition of imbalance shifted from retreat into his "spiritual world" to violent confrontation with the social world. The pattern continued until he found himself without friends.

It was his Kung Fu teacher, more than anyone else, who made him aware of his mean, antisocial behavior. Raymond had felt uncomfortable about his inability to maintain friendships, but he justified his cruel behavior by blaming a cruel world. His teacher, however, insisted that the fault lay as much in his personality.

Believing that Raymond's untoward behavior had something to do with fear of death, his Kung Fu teacher had Raymond beaten up. In the midst of his beating, Raymond had another out-of-body experience. The effect of the experience made him lose his fear of death and persuaded him to begin a serious spiritual search.

Like many others, Raymond entered his spiritual career by joining and leaving numerous groups, among them Pentecostals, Baptists, Scientologists, Krishnas, Buddhists, and others. He took some of his guidance from such occult practices as palm and tarot card reading. Finally, to overcome his hatred of rich people, he began socializing with various local politicians.

At age twenty-five he began having spiritual experiences that dealt more with a sense of mission. Disembodied voices and apparitions would tell him to "come and save us." At a strenuous session of Kung Fu training in the wintry mountains of Canada, he had a vision of cosmic importance. The world changed suddenly and became surrounded with light. He knew that something was about to happen. These experiences continued. Sipping a cup of coffee, Raymond told us that a stranger had walked up to him and asked "Would you give your life for the world?"

Everything he described subsequently consisted of coincidences into which he read great meaning. He felt strongly that he must leave the farm on which he was a laborer. One day later it was hit by a hurricane. Then he heard a distinct voice tell him to "go sit on that bench and a blonde will come and speak to you." She came, and she was wearing a watch that counted hours in colors, which he had also foreseen. The young woman talked to him of God. Coincidences continued until he joined a controversial new religion: the New Dispensation Church.

Since then, he has had to work hard to reduce his aggression. Raymond said that each morning God would speak to him in a very specific way, telling him that he had "to develop a parental heart for others by accepting the right of three different people today to have a different viewpoint" from his own. God was working on his personality, Raymond told us, showing him what it means to become a brother in the New Dispensation family.

During a bout of sickness, Raymond had further revelations about the fall of man, having an "unconditional heart," and being objective toward God. At the time, he said, he entered the spirit world, and "the spirits gave testimony to the Promise." He also had a vision of a golden city, a new Jerusalem, in which the Promise given by the leader of the New Dispensation was about to be realized. He went to a Promise ceremony and was betrothed to a wife.

To this day, Raymond is still struggling with aggression, bitterness, and suspicion, and with his excessive spiritual openness.

Poppie: Looking for Relationships

Poppie's story is shorter and less complex than Raymond's. She was born in 1955 into a working-class home in England. Her family's Anglican affiliation would indicate that they were aspiring toward a higher class status. Her parents scraped and saved money and sent Poppie to a private school. Her experience at this school left Poppie with considerable feelings of bitterness and constituted enough of an imbalance to become an *idee fixe*.

Having successfully completed an international secretarial course with competence in several languages, Poppie left England for Spain. At first, she told us, she associated with "leftists," because she "shared some of their bitterness." Their irresponsibility in practical matters and personal relationships, however, persuaded her to leave them.

She wanted to gain "mind power." To that end, she associated with a group called the Infinite Way. She reported that her working class background left her with little appreciation for meditation, however: "One has to do more in life than just sit around and meditate." Above all, she resented the pretensions of perfection among the other members and described them as lacking in morality and knowledge about relationships.

Considerably disturbed by the bitterness that she seemed unable to conquer, she studied journalism with the aim of entering a new career. She also practiced yoga to "purify her life" and clean up her personality. With these decisions she turned around a drifting (though dramatic) life and made it purposeful.

Experiencing some success at her new job, she set off for the Western United States in order to write articles about the American spiritual smorgasbord. Her job, it will be noted, was quite clearly geared to help her straighten out personal imbalances.

In San Francisco, she met members of the New Dispensation Church at their Center and was from the first excited about their relational dynamics. She attended one of the Church's retreats, studied its "Principle of Providence" at another church camp for three weeks, spent eight weeks in the Actioneers, and ended by witnessing in another city for nearly two years. Appropriately enough, she worked in the city's Spanish district, distributing food and teaching. When her visa expired, she returned to Britain, where she worked for an oil company while remaining a member of the New Dispensation Church. The following year she came to Canada.

Tim: The Rational Quest

Tim was born in 1955 to parents who were both scientists working in an agricultural community. All four children of this family were very bright. Tim told us that he skipped a grade and took university math by correspondence while still in high school. He was verbally facile and extroverted and had a sense of humor that he used primarily to defend himself, shock others, and generally to gain attention. He was clumsy in expressing his emotions, which made him appear to be somewhat insensitive.

Tim appeared to have experienced the world and his relationships in it as castrating. Significantly, he remembers an incident in the fourth grade in which four boys ganged up on him and attempted to castrate him. The emotional void in his life is perhaps best understood when one takes seriously his claim that when he told his parents of the fearful incident, they suggested that he probably did something to deserve it.

The intellectual atmosphere in his home left Tim with a feeling of inner hollowness that was only worsened by the hostility he experienced from his peers. The other children, all from an agricultural environment, appeared to be more robust and less intellectual than he.

The pervasive alienation of his school years persisted. During his second year in college, he developed chronic back problems. His first bout with this ailment left him bedridden for six weeks. He was, however, beginning to realize some benefits from his verbal skills. He reports that he was able to dissuade four individuals from committing suicide. This gift convinced him that there was a mission for him somewhere.

As we will see later, Tim is an example of a person with a hysterical personality. Such individuals characteristically describe their relationships to others and the world in repetitive, impulsive, and stereotyped ways, and they often exhibit a peculiar fascination with the occult. Tim's repetitive reference to the number *four* is a significant point in this regard. He grew up in a family of four children. Four boys ganged up on him in the fourth grade. And four times he saved someone from suicide. At the age of twenty-four he had major conflicts with a New Dispensation Church leader who was also twenty-four years old. Before he joined the New Dispensation Church the fourth and final time, he prayed for twelve minutes each night for forty nights to discover whether his decision was right.

As is common among those with a hysterical personality, Tim spoke of his relations and experiences in a stylized manner. He characteristically described stereotypical child-parent and victim-aggressor relationships. Rescue themes were common. He also produced fantasy-like explanations of situations that entailed caricature-like roles for himself and others. His relationship to his parents turned him into a victim, a theme replayed throughout his short life. There was the aggressor-victim theme with his peers in high school. Inside the New Dispensation Church, he felt victimized by what he called "middle-management leaders," which he cited as the reason he left the Church the second time.

He met a new leader named Taylor when he attended the Church's Great Lakes Center, and he said that a talk with Taylor saved him. He rejoined the church as "Taylor's chauffeur" and for a short period completely idolized the leader, referring to him as a saving master from whom flowed a healing love. In the end, however, the relationship soured. Tim sank into depression and was plagued by a recurrence of his chronic backache. He left the New Dispensation Church again, returned to college, and got a degree in industrial engineering.

While he was in school, Tim was given the assignment of analyzing interactions in a store. He chose to do so in terms of the New Dispensation Church's "Principle of Providence." He assigned the role of Esau to the store owner, the role of Lucifer to the store manager, and assumed the role of Jacob himself. In his construction of the situation, the store manager stood between him and the store owner. (Tim had always had problems with what he called "middle managers"—people who stood between himself and his master.) It was his perception that while the Jacob-Esau relationship between the owner and him flourished, Lucifer (the store manager) was driven by such jealousy as to nearly destroy the business. Apparently this psychodrama, staged in large part by Tim himself, granted him some insight. He realized that he acted wrongly toward "middle management leaders."

Unable to reach a decision about whether to return to the New Dispensation Church, he set up various tests that might help "strike him" with what to do. The forty days of prayer failed to provide him with any clear guidance, so he formulated a second test, and then a third, and a fourth. During the third test, he opened the Bible randomly and was struck by the passage he happened upon: "Again I will be your God and you will be my people." He considered this a great revelation, and he felt that the message was confirmed the next week, when he had a series of great dreams about God, Christ, and the founder of the New Dispensation Church.

Interestingly enough, this period seems to have resulted in some healing for Tim. He reported that "for the first time God had become real and personal, and I could relate to him intimately." He experienced the love of God, and the great emotional void in his life was at last filled. He also lost his fixation with cult figures and Lucifer-like middle management types.

Earlier in his career with the New Dispensation Church, Tim had had a vision "about developing Third-World industry for the sake of the Third World itself." Now he found the courage to relate that vision to others and act upon it. Several of his personal problems neared resolution. He opened a printing business to develop his business skills for the benefit of the Third World. Quite appropriately, he became engaged to a Jamaican. Then he had a tumor removed from his knee, which seemed to clear up his back problem as well.

Tim still remembers dreaming major dreams two or three times a year, and he usually uses them as an aid to solving major dilemmas. He also has visions of strange animals coming toward him. When they are sinister, he strengthens his prayer.

Brian: Emotional Confusion

In psychological terms, Brian suffers from an antisocial personality disorder, a disorder that is, in varying degrees of severity, quite common among males who join new religions. He was born out of wedlock in 1961. His natural father left during the pregnancy, and Brian never knew him. Sometime later, his mother married a man who then adopted Brian. They had four other children together. Brian's adoptive father beat him and his mother frequently. Their home was the source of constant emotional chaos. Brian remembers experiencing peace only when his grandparents took him to Sunday School.

Brian did not learn that he had been adopted until he was twelve, when his adoptive father left the family. He says that learning that the man who had beaten him all those years was not even his real father infuriated him, making him a "seedbed of hatred." He vowed to kill the man and plotted for three years to do so.

Where his adopted father was violent, his mother was weak. She was quite unable to maintain discipline. Brian and the other children learned nothing about emotions from their parents except how to vent them violently. Brian had always taken after his adoptive father, and after the man left he became even more wild. He put another child "into the hospital." He started taking heroin, but then "changed to speed [methamphetamine] because it was less expensive." Brian's mother complained that both he and his two step-brothers "were out of control."

Since his mother was unable to control the boys, Brian's adoptive father was given custody of them when Brian was fourteen. He stayed with the man for two years, which he describes as "absolute hell." He reports that there were "constant physical fights between father and me."

Brian went to jail three times, primarily for theft and forgery. He lost hope that he would ever reform and "prayed and cried to God to reveal himself." The degree of his unhappiness with his violence is evident in the fact that he instructed a friend outside to buy a gun he could use to do away with himself if he had not reformed within two and a half years, the length of his last jail sentence.

After three months in jail, Brian met a member of the New Dispensation Church who was also imprisoned. Brian says that he learned something about a spiritual life from this man. He did not, however, undergo a transformation (nor has he yet). Instead, he continued "to drink, smoke, and swear." The jail psychiatrist did, however, help him come to terms with his hatred for his father. When Brian left jail, he had a reunion with him, and he says that both he and his father "opened up and cried." His former hate for his father was not so much dissipated as redirected. When he learned that his psychiatrist had told his father about his wish to kill him, he felt betrayed and experienced an urge "to kill the psychiatrist."

Brian went to stay at a New Dispensation Church Center, but he did not have an easy time there. He resented the discipline and tried to avoid witnessing. It was suggested that he move out and return to school. Within six months, he realized that he had fallen back into the old destructive pattern. He asked to move back to the Center. Since his return he has done primarily manual labor on the farm or at the Center.

At the time of the interview, Brian was still struggling. There has been no dramatic transformation of his personality, although he has become more self-aware. He recognizes that he is "unstable" and that he "stretches the truth," and he is aware of his "volatile temper." He claims to be "repulsed by the idea of violence," however, and says that he "could never hurt anyone again." On the other hand, some Church members who live with Brian reported that "he doesn't really love God, but he sure hates Satan."

Brian reports feeling particularly close to two members of the New Dispensation Church and says that their closeness and warmth steady him. So does fantasy. He reports that he loves science fiction movies and books by Tolkien, LeGuin, and Donaldson, among others. His violence, once directed toward specific people, seems to have undergone a transformation. It is now his aspiration to play a central role in "the triumph over communism." Words and acts that once made him violent now make him laugh.

Brian's growth is slow and arduous. Far from being spiritual, except as a voyeur, he is only learning to diversify his narrowly focused and violent emotions. He has added "warmth," "openness," "willingness to be vulnerable," "fantasy," and "laughter" to a catalogue of emotions once restricted principally to hatred.

EXPERIENCE, MYTH, AND IDEOLOGY

So far we have argued that the new mythology predisposes individuals to accept the outlook of new religious movements and that primal experiences give the mythology a life of its own. But in and of themselves, the new mythology and primal experiences are simply unorganized material. They are vivid and enchanting, but they do not lead to any specific destination. Each new religious group has its own ideology, and it is this ideology that distinguishes it from all other groups.

A good example of fact that the new mythology cannot by itself provide direction to a group, even when it is reinforced by repeated primal experiences, is the religious community that formed near the town of Glastonbury in England in the mid-1960s and early 1970s. A variety of English and American hippies came together in this setting because of its rich mythological background, incorporating medieval legends about King Arthur and Jesus. Individuals gave many reports of encounters with King Arthur, Hobbits, Jesus, and a variety of other figures, and yet no organized movement developed.

The early Findhorn Community headed by Peter Caddy was similarly rich in primal experiences, but it too had no definite ideology. Only after the arrival of David Spengler did the Community develop a distinct ideology based on a combination of futurism and various eastern philosophies. Later still, in the early 1980s, the Findhorn group obtained property in Glastonbury and proceeded to propagate a unified ideology.

Even if they support vivid primal experiences and rich eclectic mythologies, groups like the early Glastonbury and Findhorn communities will not coalesce into new religious movements unless they can draw upon some established theological or ideological framework to give structure to both the experiences and the myths. We should turn next, then, to a closer look at the sources of these overarching frameworks.

6

The Yogic and
Abramic Traditions

In addition to primal experiences and the new mythology, new religions have incorporated doctrines from world religions to give intellectual content to their beliefs. At first glance it might appear that there are hundreds if not thousands of religious traditions in the world. But upon closer examination, we see that all of the world's religions fall into the categories of two major traditions. We call these traditions Yogic and Abramic.

The best-known religions of the Yogic tradition are Jainism, Hinduism, and Buddhism. Those of the Abramic are Judaism, Christianity, and Islam. We use the term "Yogic" because the practice of yoga represents the strand of this complex tradition that most influences new religions in the West. The term Abramic has been used to describe Judaism, Christianity, and Islam because these religions trace their origins to Abraham.

The discussion of Yogic and Abramic beliefs that follows is aimed at producing a typology for understanding new religions in Western societies. It is not meant to be a description of "pure" or historic versions of world religions. We are simply presenting some aspects of religious belief that are commonly found in new religions.

YOGIC RELIGIONS

The Yogic tradition originated in India. Themes of quest and pilgrimage are key features of its pointedly transcendental emphasis. Philosophically, Yogic religions assume this world to be a veil of sorrow that must be endured and escaped. A. C. Bhaktivedanta Swami Prabhupada (henceforth called Prabhupada), the founder of the Hare Krishna movement, sums up the negativity of the Yogic tradition when he says of the world that "this place is not meant for happiness. . . . It is a place of miseries and . . . is temporary."[1] Similarly, Edward Conze writes that "the Buddhist point of view will appeal only to those people who are completely disillusioned with the world as it is, and with themselves, who are extremely sensitive to pain, suffering, and any kind of turmoil, who have an extreme desire for happiness, and a considerable capacity for renunciation. . . . The buddhist seeks for a total happiness beyond this world."[2] As we have noted, these perspectives are common among those who join new religions.

To most Westerners, the Yogic view of the human condition seems extremely pessimistic, but practitioners of Yogic religions would disagree. Mircea Eliade, for example, has stated that Yogic soteriological doctrines "may appear 'pessimistic' to Westerners, for whom personality remains, in the last analysis, the foundation of all morality and mysticism. But, for India, what matters most is not so much the salvation of the *personality* as obtaining *absolute freedom*."[3] Yogic religions portray a very different sort of salvation than do Abramic religions. The latter place primary value on human personality and emphasize the salvation of the individual, while Yogic religions speak of salvation *away from* individuality. As Ninian Smart has written, Yogic thinking holds that

> men and other living beings are continually being reborn. With death, the individual is reborn in a different form. This everlasting recurrence of births and deaths can only be stopped by transcending it by attaining a liberation in a transcendental sphere where the self is freed from mental and bodily encumbrances. Typically, this is achieved by the practice of austerity and yoga: self-denial and self-discipline are means of destroying that which leads to rebirth—Karma.[4]

---

[1]Prabhupada, *The Search for Liberation* (Los Angeles: Bhaktivedanta Book Trust, 1982), p. 10.

[2]Conze, *Buddhism* (New York: Harper & Row, 1959), p. 22.

[3]Eliade, *Yoga, Immortality and Freedom* (London: Routledge & Kegan Paul, 1969), p. 35.

[4]Smart, *Religious Experience of Mankind* (New York: Scribner's, 1969), p. 70.

What exactly is karma, and what role does it and other key doctrines play in the new religious consciousness of the West?

KARMA

Belief in karma is the key to understanding Yogic beliefs in Western society. At its crudest, karma is viewed as a physical substance that literally sticks to people's souls, binding them to the material world. Karma is the cosmic law of cause and effect that ensures that whatever a person does, good or bad, has ultimate consequences. If we do good, we produce good karma. If we do evil, we produce bad karma. Good karma frees us from the illusions of the material world and makes liberation possible. Bad karma binds us to life and creates illusions of happiness.

The source of Yogic belief in karma is the ancient *Brhadaranyaka Upanisad,* which says that "according as one acts, according as one conducts himself, so does he become. The doer of good becomes good. The doer of evil becomes evil. One becomes virtuous by virtuous action, bad by bad action." In the foreword to his translation of the *Bhagavadgita,* Prabhupada explains the action of karma as follows:

> Suppose I am a businessman and have worked very hard with intelligence and have amassed a great bank balance. Then I am an enjoyer. But then say I have lost all my money in business; then I am a sufferer. Similarly, in every field of life we enjoy the results of our works, or we suffer the results. This is called karma.[5]

In the West, Madame Blavatsky was the first to extend the idea of karma from the realm of personal fortune to that of global events. In *The Key to Theosophy* she writes,

> We must not lose sight of the fact that every atom is subject to the general law governing the whole body to which it belongs, and here we come upon the wider track of Karmic law. Do you not perceive that the aggregate of individual karma becomes that of the nation to which individuals belong, and further, that the sum total of National Karma is that of the World?[6]

---

[5]*Bhagavad Gita,* trans. A. C. Bhaktivedanta (New York: Macmillan, 1968), p. xix.

[6]Blavatsky, *The Key to Theosophy* (1888; rpt., Pasadena: Theosophical University Press, 1972), p. 202.

In the counterculture of the 1960s, this theosophical understanding of the effects of karma was used to explain the Vietnam
War and later the ecological crisis. In 1971 a large, free pop festi-
val, the Glastonbury Fyere, was held in England. The organizers
said that they intended to help "reverse the bad effects of karma"
on the environment and "restore the ecological balance." Countless articles reflecting this outlook were published in such journals as *New Age* and *Co-Evolution Quarterly*. All interpret elements of the new mythology in terms of karma to produce a
strong nature mysticism.

REBIRTH

Within the Yogic tradition, ideas of rebirth are logically related to
belief in karma. Traditionally, rebirth is explained in two ways.
Hinduists believe that when human beings die, their souls pass—
"transmigrate"—into another body. Buddhists, on the other
hand, deny the existence of the soul. They believe that the continuation of sense impressions at the point of death deludes those
who suffer near-death experiences into thinking that they have an
essence or soul. Buddhists postulate reincarnation rather than
transmigration. Those who popularize new religions in the West,
however, typically fail to convey these distinctions. They tend to
define reincarnation as rebirth in human form and transmigration as rebirth in nonhuman form.
      Western belief in reincarnation typically has nothing to do
with karma. It is usually called upon as a means of explaining
claims that some people remember past lives. Past-life experiences have been widely popularized of late. Books such as Raymond
A. Moody's *Life after Life* give the impression that they are scientifically valid phenomena.[7]
      Within Yogic religions, karma and rebirth provide a power-
ful basis for social morality and offer an explanation for inequali-
ties in society. In the West, however, the moral element of these
beliefs is usually deemphasized in favor of a strong romanticism:
its popularity lies in the fact that it meets psychological rather
than moral needs. It is this sort of emphasis that accounts for the
claims in the popular literature that karma can bring lovers together or enable us to meet people we knew in previous lives.
      Many members of new religions say that they remember

---

[7]Moody, *Life after Life* (New York: Bantam, 1976).

past lives and adventures. Their "memories" give them a false sense of personal worth and enable them to escape difficult personal relationships with the excuse that they have not yet found their "soul mate." Simply put, the idea of rebirth is often used to avoid moral obligations.

For most Westerners and members of new religions, belief in reincarnation is an exciting idea that seems to offer past adventures and future hope. Few relate the idea of rebirth to the need for salvation or the possibility of being reborn in hell. Once a person makes the move from a generalized belief in reincarnation to joining a new religion of Yogic origin, the need for salvation and the implications of reincarnation and karma are quickly realized.

SAMSARA, MAYA, DHARMA, AND MOKSHA

Samsara, or the "wheel of existence," is the name given a vast network of births and deaths through endless lifetimes involving incarnations in many worlds, heavens, and hells. Those who believe in samsara assume that everything and every being are bound together in the infinite repetition of birth and death through karma.

Ordinarily people do not experience the bonds of karma or become aware of the wheel of existence. Instead they experience their individual lives as a fleeting moment of consciousness to which they ascribe ultimate significance. But this awareness of one's individuality and belief in the significance of one's present life is an illusion brought about by the effects of karma. Karma blinds us to the reality of samsara and thus to the possibility of escaping our karmic bonds and attaining liberation. Karma creates the illusion of individuality and of a permanent creation when in reality everything is in a state of constant flux. The illusory nature of our experience of reality is brought about by *maya,* which magically conjures up an unreal world. Once we see through the illusion, however, we realize that we need to be liberated from samsara and the bonds of karma.

In Hinduism, *dharma* is a religious way of life that embraces all one does and all of society. Dharma implies the idea of a fixed standard of divine conduct that is a sacred law by which human beings must live. In the West, though, dharma has come to be understood primarily in terms of its Buddhist meaning as teaching about what is right or the truth about reality. When members of new religions speak of the dharma, they will most often be referring to the way to liberation according to their own particular beliefs.

Liberation, or freedom from the bonds of karma and release from samsara, is known as *moksha*. Moksha takes many forms in Hinduism. Those who believe in it contend that it can be experienced as absorption into the whole or god, as entry into life with a particular god such as Krishna, or simply as annihilation. In Buddhism, liberation is called *nirvana*. It is said that we cannot really say what nirvana is, because it is not conditioned by our universe of cause and effect and is consequently beyond our comprehension. We can do no more than affirm our belief in it. All we can really know is that nirvana is freedom from the wheel of samsara and the bonds of karma. It is the cessation of our present mode of existence. Buddhist teaching also maintains that while we cannot explain what nirvana is, we can know what enables people to attain it.

New religions have linked ideas about nirvana and salvation generally with the concept of an evolving human consciousness. Marilyn Ferguson expresses this idea in a secular way in *The Aquarian Conspiracy*. David Spangler sacralizes it in *Emergence*. Lawrence Blair offers a self-consciously religious understanding of liberation as a higher evolutionary state in *Rhythms of Vision*. T. Lobsand Rampa, a former Bradford plumber who has claimed to be a Tibetan lama, aptly describes the importance of these ideas when he writes that "to live one has to progress. . . . Nirvana is the stage in humans where all faults are eliminated . . . the state where there is no evil."[8] To religious purists the mythologizing of Yogic beliefs in these ways may appear shocking, but they represent a common theme in the new religions.

ASTROLOGY

Many Western scholars have chosen to ignore the magical aspects of Yogic religions. Scholars such as C. A. F. Rhys-Davids in the nineteenth century and Christmas Humphreys in our own have attempted to present religions like Buddhism as the height of rationality. Other scholars, such as Conze and Eliade, have rightly drawn attention to the magical aspects of Yogic religions and particularly to the importance of belief in astrology.[9]

---

[8]Rampa, *Chapters of Life* (London: TransWorld Publishers, 1967), p. 197.

[9]For a scholarly discussion of Western attitudes to Buddhism, see Christ-

As Eliade points out, belief in astrology arises naturally from a belief in karma and rebirth. In the West, astrology is accepted today largely because people believe it works rather than because of its relationship to other beliefs. Once accepted as a reality, however, astrology naturally reinforces belief in such things as karma, and it dramatizes Yogic beliefs generally.

It is important to recognize that there are two distinct forms of astrology: natal and mundane. Natal astrology concerns individuals and their personal lives. Mundane astrology deals with cultural development and world history. The best known belief associated with mundane astrology is that of the dawning of the age of Aquarius, which is part of the new mythology.

Historically, belief in astrology was widespread in the Greco-Roman world. It declined with the rise of Christianity and was ridiculed by early Christian writers. Astrological ideas were revived during the sixteenth-century Renaissance, but they were severely criticized by both the Protestant Reformers and leaders of the Catholic Counter-Reformation. By the time of the Enlightenment in the eighteenth century, European astrology had virtually died out. In the nineteenth century, it was generally regarded as a failed science.

Outside of Europe, in India, China, and the Islamic world, astrology seems to have retained its popularity with relatively little serious criticism. In Europe, it was revived toward the end of the nineteenth century by movements such as Theosophy. Today, astrology is increasingly popular. Some forty percent of Americans say they believe in it.

Astrology is an ancient belief that has been thoroughly discredited by serious testing. Richard Cavendish documents some of these failures in his book *The Black Arts,* correctly observing that "astrology is essentially a magical art" linked to irrational beliefs and a desire to gain control over seemingly uncontrollable events.[10]

Contemporary Western interest in astrology demonstrates a deep desire for certainty in the context of a fear of the future. In

---

mas Humphries, *Sixty Years of Buddhis in Britain* (London: Buddhist Society, 1968), and Charles Prebish, *American Buddhism* (Belmont, Cal.: Duxbury Press, 1979). For a more controversial and entertaining personal account, see the autobiography of Edward Conze, *The Memoirs of a Modern Gnostic,* 2 vols. (Sherborne: Samizdat Publishing, 1979).

[10]Cavendish, *The Black Arts* (New York: G. P. Putnam, 1967), p. 219.

the Yogic tradition, astrology fits well with shamanistic practices and beliefs about human beings with superhuman powers. Within the new religions, astrology and shamanism unite to confirm the authenticity of the group's leader. Members of new religions from Scientology to the Unification Church and from the Children of God to Hare Krishna commonly appeal to astrological signs in an attempt to prove that their leader has a divine mission.

THE MEANING OF YOGA

We have noted various Yogic beliefs and mentioned the practice of yoga as unifying Yogic religions. But what is yoga? Mediators and members of new religions claim that yoga is "a way of life," "an experience," "a healthy exercise," and simply "a way of meditation." In fact all of these descriptions are correct. Eliade states that "etymologically *yoga* derives from the root *yuj*, 'to bind together,' 'hold fast,' 'yoke.' . . . The word *yoga* serves, in general, to describe any *ascetic technique* and any *method of meditation*."[11]

Meditation or yoga can be described as an inward journey on which the meditator leaves behind the rational mind and enters a new realm of consciousness. Many methods of yoga are popular today. Most of these methods involve the concentration of the mind, breathing exercises, or devotional activities such as the dances and chants of the Hare Krishna movement.

The results of meditation vary from person to person and are modified by the particular beliefs the meditator claims to hold. Generally, however, practitioners say meditation results in "enlightenment" and freedom from the confines of the everyday world. In yogic terminology, it leads to a release from the bonds of karma.

New religions offer various explanations of what one should expect in meditation. Transcendental Meditation (T.M.) teaches that meditators reach a deep peace as a result of tapping the inner resources of the human mind. Members of the Friends of the Western Buddhist Order have traditional beliefs in nirvana. Devotees of Hare Krishna talk of the glories of Krishna conscious-

---

[11]Eliade, *Yoga, Immortality and Freedom*, p. 4. Richard Hittleman admits that prior to the mid-1960s he used the idea that yoga was healthy to hook Americans and get them interested in Hindu religious ideas; see his *Guide to Yoga Meditation* (New York: Bantam Books, 1969), pp. 9-14.

ness. Other meditators speak about a sense of absorption or a loss of consciousness and bliss.

In attempting to understand how people describe meditation, it is important to note that they universally maintain that words cannot fully express the sort of liberation they experience as a result of meditating. One can experience meditation and its results, they say, but it is impossible to describe them fully to another person. What we can say with assurance is that when meditators do attempt to describe their experiences, they repeatedly depict states of consciousness we associate with primal experiences and the use of drugs.

THE YOGIC SYSTEM

Central to Yogic beliefs is the acceptance of a holistic vision of the universe that incorporates an evolutionary perspective, which gives it an apparent scientific validity. Behind this vision is an assumption that the whole of reality is ultimately *one* and that our material world is really illusory because the true reality is on a different, nonmaterial plane.

The version of the Yogic tradition found in the West is more unified and clear-cut in its monism than is Eastern Yogic philosophy. Many of the schools of philosophy in India, Japan, and other Eastern nations do propound the essential oneness of everything—nondualism, as it is known in the Indian philosophic tradition. But elements of materialism and other views are also strong in the Indian tradition. The preeminence of the Upanishads, the philosophy of Sankara, and Buddhism in the Western perception of Eastern religions has led Westerners to assume that nondualism constitutes the essence of Yogic thinking.

Steven M. Tipton sums up the worldview of the Western Yogic tradition as follows:

> Mixed meanings make up the world in which the counterculture's individual lives, and a mixed moral logic governs her actions in it. Conceptions of the divine, where they exist, tend to be nontheistic or at least they describe a nonprophetic sort of god who issues no commandments. Nor is the countercultural universe a cosmos structured by natural law or philosophic principle in the usual Western sense. Instead, there is the fundamental assumption of an acosmic monism, that "all is one," pure energy or existence without any enduring structure or *logos*. This monism constitutes the fundamental difference in cognitive

orientation between the counterculture and utilitarian culture, which is predicated on philosophical realism or dualism.[12]

This difference between the counterculture and the culture at large is also reflected, notes Tipton, in the counterculture's "rejection of the conventional Christian outlook."

Salvation in the Western Yogic tradition is a matter of overcoming our awareness of dualism and individualism in order to experience oneness. Thus, it conceives of the human plight as essentially an ontological problem, a matter of our fundamental way of being and our belief in individualism. We are delivered when we lose our identity as individuals and our consciousness of personhood. As Eliade puts it, "the wretchedness of human life is not owing to divine punishment or to an original sin, but to *ignorance* ... metaphysical ignorance."[13] Life is wretched because we experience it as separation, and we will continue to do so until we understand and experience the oneness of all things, until we merge with the Absolute.

Practitioners of yoga maintain that the discipline is the essential means by which one can regain one's true ontological status and lose individual personhood. But yoga is difficult. One needs the instruction of a guru.

THE GURU

All those who write about yoga maintain that serious meditation requires a guide, or guru. Yogic practices produce trances or similar psychological states that could easily harm the uninitiated without the protection of one who is more experienced.

The guru is a person who has already been initiated into the spiritual world and is therefore able to help the uninitiated. Eliade discusses the historic relationship between the guru and the shaman. Peter Brent gives a more vivid account of gurus in his book *Godmen of India*.[14] He shows that the guru demands an inflexible relationship in which his disciples surrender totally to his authority. Gurus teach and facilitate. They have gone before and experienced the terrors of psychological disorientation that med-

---

[12]Tipton, *Getting Saved from the Sixties: Moral Meaning in Conversion and Cultural Change* (Berkeley and Los Angeles: University of California Press, 1981), p. 14.

[13]Eliade, *Yoga, Immortality and Freedom*, p. 14.

[14]Brent, *Godmen of India* (Harmondsworth: Penguin, 1973).

itation can bring. In the language of Yogic religion, the guru encounters spiritual beings, battles demons, and embraces gods.
Each guru shares a tradition with other gurus and none speaks for
him- or herself. Each guru has his or her own guru, living or dead,
so that a succession of teachers share esoteric knowledge and
communicate ancient techniques of psychic manipulation.

Gurus are not prophets who declare the will of God and appeal to propositions found in a Scripture. Rather, they are said to
be greater than God because they lead to God. Gurus have shared
the essence of the Absolute and experienced the oneness of being,
which endows them with divine powers and the ability to master
people and things in this world.

In India the true guru is held to be a god-man with superhuman powers and is recognized as a sacred being. But in the West
there is a clear distinction between the explicit and implicit
claims to divinity of contemporary gurus. L. Ron Hubbard of Scientology did not explicitly claim divine status, but it is clear from
the way committed Scientologists speak that they regarded him
as more than human. Similarly, Werner Erhard, the founder of
EST, claims simply to have discovered a way to make life work
better through a technique of humanistic psychology. Outsiders
report, however, that in Erhard's presence his followers clearly
treat him as though he were a divine being.

At the other end of the spectrum are the followers of
Prabhupada, who claim that their deceased guru has ascended to
the spiritual world, where he has become a god. Members of the
Divine Light Mission went even further. They declared that their
leader, the thirteen-year-old Guru Maharaj Ji, was a living god.

Standing between the god figure and the prophet are individuals such as the Reverend Moon, who is presumed to be
semidivine, with spiritual power and holy missions. Members of
the Unification Church do not believe that Moon is a god, but they
do believe that he is more than a mere prophet. For them he is the
Lord of the Second Advent. He has become a Christ figure by assuming the office of the messiah and fulfilling God's will on earth.
To understand the difference between the guru and the prophet,
we will have to investigate the Abramic tradition, in which the
idea of prophet originated.

THE ABRAMIC TRADITION

Abramic religions trace their ancestry to the person of Abraham
whose story is recorded in the Hebrew scriptures. The major reli-

gions of this tradition are Judaism, Christianity, and Islam, which have a common understanding of God as Creator. They also share such related concepts as creation, fall, redemption, and revelation. The meanings of these doctrines differ somewhat from one religion to the next. Because we wish to understand new religions in Western society, we will concentrate on the Christian interpretation of the Abramic tradition, because today's new Abramic religions principally draw their ideas from Christianity, particularly Protestant Christianity.[15]

There are new religious movements among Jews and Muslims, Roman Catholics and Eastern Orthodox Christians, but they are for the most part revitalization movements that essentially remain faithful to the tradition from which they arose. The Protestant equivalent of these new types of orthodox religions is Christian fundamentalism rather than groups like the Moonies, The Way, or the Children of God. We will not be focussing on fundamentalism or any of the new religions that affirm a traditional form of religious orthodoxy.

THE DOCTRINE OF CREATION

The doctrine of creation sets Abramic religions apart from Yogic religions. Following the Hebrew Bible, Abramic religions teach that God brought the entire universe into existence by an act of will. He did not reform already-existing matter or change a part of himself to make material things. Rather, "what is seen was not made out of what was visible" (Heb. 11:3). As the Nicene Creed states, God is "the Creator of heaven and earth, and of all things visible and invisible."

But the Abramic tradition conceives of creation as far more than just an original creative act that started the universe. The scriptures of the Abramic religions—the Judeo-Christian Bible and the Islamic Koran—construe creation as involving God's *continuing* providence as well. They assert that God made the worlds and continues to uphold them by his will, which is expressed in terms of law. God rules the universe by his law, which governs every aspect of life. If God were to cease to will the continuation of all things, they would cease to exist.

---

[15]For a more detailed discussion of basic Protestant Christian beliefs than appears in the following outline, we would recommend study of Calvin's *Institutes of the Christian Religion*, W. H. Griffith Thomas's *Principles of Theology* (London: Longmans, Green, 1930), and Carl F. H. Henry's *God, Revelation and Authority*, 4 vols. (Waco, Tex.: Word Books, 1976).

The Abramic religions all contend that God is not dependent on the universe but that the universe is dependent upon God,
that God is the sovereign ruler of the universe and everything is
subordinate to him. God is absolute, and everything else is relative. We owe our existence to God; as created beings, we are finite, while God is infinite. There is, therefore, an absolute distinction between the creature and the Creator.

Another important aspect of the Abramic doctrine of creation is that when God created the universe, he pronounced it to
be good. Abramic religions agree that God's original creation was
without blemish. They also agree that the present state of human
alienation from God and the presence of evil and suffering in the
world were not part of God's original intention. It resulted from
an act of human will that had cosmic implications: the fall.

THE FALL

The Abramic religions differ in their understanding of the fall and
God's subsequent acts of redemption. The basis for Christian interpretations of the fall is found in chapters two and three of the
book of Genesis, which relate the story of the garden of Eden.
Adam was told that he could eat of any tree except the "tree of the
knowledge of good and evil" because "in the day that thou eatest
thereof thou shalt surely die." Then the serpent entered the story
and convinced Adam and Eve that eating the forbidden fruit
would not lead to death but would make them into gods "knowing
good and evil." They ate, discovered their mistake, and lost communication with God. Death entered the world.

Setting aside the issue of the historicity of this story, what
does it teach us about the human condition? Adam and Eve were
given freedom within the limits of human finitude and were
placed in an ideal environment. They were warned about the danger of death but were otherwise left alone to explore the world.
The serpent then urged them to ignore God's warning. Since animals do not normally talk, the story might be suggesting that
human beings were misled by their senses into doubting God.

The central theme in the story is distrust. Adam and Eve desire the "knowledge of good and evil" that would make them "like
God." This suggests not only that they were discontent with their
dependent status as finite creatures but also that they desired independence from God through knowledge gained by the ritual
act of eating rather than through growth and thought. If this interpretation is correct, the story symbolizes the ever-present human

desire for magical short-cuts to knowledge and power at the expense of trust and understanding.

At the heart of the fall is the human desire for sudden and total freedom and power, unrestricted by the limits of the human condition. As we have seen, this is precisely what the Yogic religions claim to offer their followers. The Bible presents the fall as an act of unrestricted self-indulgence based on the impossible desire to be like God. Instead of leading to freedom, it results in bondage.

Following the fall, material things rather than personal relationships come to dominate mankind's existence. The desire for power disrupts human relationships. Distrust of God leads to distrust of human neighbors, and anxiety about life leads to a continued search for the means to control other people. After the fall, humanity is marked by a magical understanding of the world and a desire to manipulate knowledge in a manner indistinguishable from sorcery. If this were the end of the story, our plight as humans would be sad indeed. But the Bible goes on to say that after the fall God took active steps to restore the relationship between humankind and himself. These steps are known as redemption.

REDEMPTION

Together with the fall, the incarnation and resurrection of Jesus are the central doctrines of the Christian faith. For the purposes of this discussion, we can say that they form a major Christian theological unit defining God and man. If the actions of Adam and Eve broke the trust between man and God, God restored it with the birth and death of Jesus. In the process, human beings learned who they are: finite creatures who nevertheless have a freedom of choice. And we learned who God is: a being both infinite and divine.

As we noted earlier, mistrust entered the relationship between humanity and God in the fall. God became suspect. To redeem us from suspicion and regression, God redeemed himself with an act of infinite love. He gave us Jesus, leaving us free to choose our attitude and relationship to him. Reflection on the fact that we chose to crucify him might have left us wallowing in guilt, but by resurrecting him, God not only redeemed us but also showed us that he is infinite. God redeemed us by redeeming himself at the same time that he defined us as distinct and different from himself, subject to his divinity yet free in our humanity.

The Christian notion of redemption, as we interpret it in this admittedly limited way, fits well with Western attitudes toward science and knowledge. It grants us knowledge and choice within the confines of God's universe but dictates that since we are not granted ultimate or God-like knowledge, our pursuit of knowledge can never be complete. It does not allow us to rest in the comfort of having attained union with the One as the believers of Eastern religions do, but it thereby prevents us from stagnation. Its emphasis is not on *being* (except in the sense of being at peace) but rather on *becoming*. It entails that the pursuit of knowledge and exploration is never-ending for humanity, that we will always be able to experience growth, development, and above all hope.

Nor does the Christian sense of becoming have anything necessarily to do with evolution, especially not with the myth of evolution. Our becoming may be regressive or progressive, good or bad. This central Christian theme assures us that we were given the wherewithal to build and destroy and the opportunity to choose whether to build or destroy. It leaves us with the hope of finding ever new frontiers to conquer, without the delusion that all "conquest" will be ipso facto "higher" and "better." The paths we travel are a matter of our choosing. These Christian doctrines leave us with a feeling of exhilaration, for they indicate that we have the opportunity to direct all that God has given us. And we can do so without having to hallucinate spirit helpers. Choice is conscious, not fortuitous, not subject to the occult, not even subject to a belief in the evil powers of humanity. It allows us to act in the world from the healthy perspective of trust.

THE IMPORTANCE OF FAITH

Christians believe that the way humans reenter a living relationship with God is through faith. Faith is an act of trust based upon knowledge of God and his deeds. It is not a blind leap into the unknown but a confident step into enlightenment about the nature and love of God. Faith is the opposite of doubt and magical power. Faith is to redemption what magic and doubt are to the fall. It frees us of anxiety because it entails our accepting our identity as creatures made in God's image.

The inspiration for the distinctively Christian understanding of faith is found in the story of Abraham, who left the security of Ur of the Chaldees to become a wanderer and nomad in response to God's call (see Gen. 12-24 and Heb. 11:8-19). Theistic faith is an expression of trust. It leads to a new way of life based on a living relationship with God.

The longest exposition in the Bible of the meaning of faith is found in the book of Romans. It starts with Paul's observation that people have renounced truth and served "the creature more than the Creator." The essence of Paul's argument is that human beings, having lost the ability to trust God, made gods out of created things. In so doing, they lost the ability to trust each other, with disastrous results. But faith restores not only our relationship with God but also our relationship with our neighbors.

Unfortunately, it is difficult to have faith. Many people choose to be satisfied with the sort of apparent reconciliation to God and neighbors that can be achieved by observing rigid codes, ritual actions, and prescribed ways of living. They look to laws rather than faith for instruction concerning how all people must live. These laws appear to restore human relationships and create communion with God, but in fact they produce a new kind of servitude. Paul calls this servitude "legalism" and discusses it at length in Galatians.

Legalism leads to magical practices and the observance of "feasts, sacred days, and sabbaths," which are justified by appeals to what Paul calls "philosophy and vain deceit after the tradition of men" (Col. 2:8, 16). The "law" also includes such things as observing genealogies, continuing ancient rituals such as circumcision, and keeping dietary rules. Paul and other New Testament writers condemn all of these ritual observances, denouncing them as bondage (see Acts 10; 15:1-29; Gal. 2-4; 1 Tim. 1:4).

In Galatians 3:1 Paul describes people who have submitted to legalism as "bewitched." Usually we regard this phrase as a figure of speech. When read in conjunction with Galatians 5:20, however, in which "witchcraft" is classified with idolatry and other sins as "the works of the flesh," a different interpretation suggests itself. In Paul's view, legalism is akin to bewitchment and is, therefore, nothing other than the power of sorcery.

In the Christian tradition, faith is presumed to free people to enter meaningful, nonexploitative relationships, whereas legalism is presumed to create dependence, addiction, and exploitation. The essence of legalism is the replacement of trust in God with manipulation through rituals. Legalism is therefore the continual reenactment of the fall.[16]

---

[16]For a good discussion of this point, see D. Martyn Lloyd-Jones, *Spiritual Depression: Its Cause and Its Cure* (Grand Rapids: Eerdmans, 1984).

As Steven Tipton points out, one of the reasons the counter-culture and new religions have grown is that many young people have turned to them after having rejected the legalism of Christian churches. Ironically, however, by joining new religions, they enter even more repressive and legalistic situations. In effect, they are simply exchanging one form of legalism for another.

CREATION, FALL, REDEMPTION, AND NEW RELIGIONS

The new religious movements that grow out of the Abramic tradition typically deny the necessity of a faith relationship in favor of new forms of legalism. Biblical views of creation, which view the material world as good, are replaced by quasi-Yogic conceptions of the world as evil. Groups such as the Local Church have developed spirituality to the point that salvation of the soul becomes the sole objective in life. The traditional Christian emphasis on "glorifying God" and enjoying his creation is lost, and practices are introduced that encourage mystical visions that deny bodily experiences.

Many new religions find sexuality problematic. The Unification Church, for example, explains the fall in terms of wrongful sex. The church seeks to redeem sex, however, by staging elaborate shamanistic marriage rituals. Other groups shun sex altogether or conversely maintain that it is the means to ultimate liberation. Both of these emphases subvert the biblical vision of human beings as the image bearers of God. They lead couples who should be concentrating their efforts on establishing a loving relationship to focus it instead on the desire to escape this world.

THE RETURN OF CHRIST

Ideas about the "return of Christ" give many new religions their distinctive emphasis. These ideas arise out of the interpretation of the eschatological passages of the Bible, such as those in the books of Daniel and Revelation as well as key passages in the Gospels such as Matthew 24. Attempting to understand the "true" meaning of prophetic passages in the Bible, new religious movements ignore established methods of exegesis and often use novel interpretive tools. For example, Charles Taze Russell, the founder of the Jehovah's Witnesses, found in the Great Pyramid of Egypt "sacred measurements" that he believed unlocked the "meaning" of the Bible.

The key to this type of esoteric interpretation is the magical manipulation of numbers. In essence it involves ways of thinking that display an obsession with coincidence and the creation of sacred patterns. Such ways of viewing the world are typical of people under severe stress or those who are suffering from hysteria. Anton T. Boisen has also observed that an obsession with impending doom is common among mentally disturbed individuals.[17]

TYPES OF ESCHATOLOGY

To understand the ways in which new religions develop their ideas about the return of Christ, we need to look more closely at traditional Christian eschatological teachings. There are three basic theological understandings of biblical eschatology: postmillennialism, premillennialism, and amillennialism. For our purposes, it will only be necessary to look at the first two.

The postmillennialist position and its variations is the more orthodox, being held by the majority of Christians throughout history. It holds that the gospel must be preached to every nation, after which there will be a thousand years of peace before Christ returns to judge men and nations. The Puritans held a particularly optimistic version of this view, maintaining that the millennium would be a period of continuous progress and human advancement.

The premillennialist position has had few supporters throughout church history, achieving popularity only as recently as the nineteenth century. Today it represents the dominant mode of interpretation in North America. One of the best-known presentations of this position is Hal Lindsey's book *The Late Great Planet Earth*.

Essentially, premillennialists believe that society will disintegrate into chaos before the second coming of Christ. Instead of a thousand years of peace, there will be universal unrest and widespread persecution of Christians. In recent years this view has been directly linked with the expectation of atomic war, because the New Testament speaks of the world being destroyed by fire (2 Pet. 3:10).

Dispensationalism is a variation of premillennialism that was popularized by the *Scofield Bible* (1917) and is taught at such

---

[17]Boisen, *The Exploration of the Inner World: A Study of Mental Disorder and Religious Experience* (1936; Philadelphia: University of Pennsylvania Press, 1971).

places as the influential Dallas Theological Seminary. Dispensationalism adopts the basic premillennial scheme but divides history into seven time periods, or dispensations, during which God is said to have dealt with humanity on the basis of different expectations and offered different ways of obtaining salvation.

An important issue on which postmillennialists and premillennialists disagree is the biblical teaching about Israel. Premillennialists contend that biblical references to Israel are references to the Jewish people. They maintain that the return of the Jewish people to Palestine and the establishment of the state of Israel in 1948 was a fulfillment of biblical prophecy. Consequently, they are strongly pro-Israel. More importantly, they expect a battle between Israel and the Arab nations and/or Russia to signal the end of the world.

Postmillennialists reject this type of interpretation, maintaining that the Jews who returned to Palestine cannot be identified with the biblical nation of Israel, which was destroyed in the sixth century B.C. The Jews who subsequently returned to Palestine are not really the people of Israel, they argue. They are descendants of the tribe of Judah.

Postmillennialists also argue that the references to the nation of Israel in New Testament prophecies are in fact references to the church of Christ. The reference to Israel in Hebrew scripture cited in 1 Peter 2:9, for instance, is meant to be applied to Christians, and when Paul ponders the fate of Israel in Romans 9-11, he is referring to the church, the new Israel into which God has "grafted" Gentiles (see especially Rom. 11:13-24).

THE EFFECTS OF ESCHATOLOGY

To many people arguments about eschatology may seem unimportant. But many new religious movements cannot be understood apart from their eschatological beliefs. The notorious Children of God began as a premillennialist, fundamentalist sect. They believed that the end of the world was imminent and that their leader, David Berg, had had visions confirming it. Acting on their belief, they adopted an itinerant lifestyle and lived as a people waiting for the end. Many of their excesses can be understood in the light of the urgency their premillennialism created.[18]

---

[18]For a balanced discussion of eschatology, see Steven Travis, *The Jesus Hope* (Waco, Tex.: Word Books, 1974).

By contrast, the Unification Church espouses a traditional postmillennial eschatology, contending that a thousand years of peace must precede the day of judgment. They are optimistic about the future and work exceptionally hard to usher in the era of peace. Their political, business, and other activities are intended to be steps towards creating a heavenly kingdom on earth in keeping with their postmillennialist eschatology.

ESCHATOLOGY AND CHARISMATIC GIFTS

The eschatology of the Abramic tradition has also given rise to significant prophetic and charismatic movements. Christians who call themselves "charismatics" believe that glossolalia ("speaking in tongues"), healing the sick, prophecy, and other "gifts of the Spirit" are signs of "the last days." Verses from Acts 2, John 14-16, and many other passages of Scripture are used to justify such expectations.

In the 1960s, books such as David Wilkerson's *The Cross and the Switchblade* and John L. Sherrill's *They Speak with Other Tongues* popularized the notion that God's Spirit is at work today in preparation for the end.[19] The implications of these beliefs are that established, noncharismatic, churches are spiritually dead and that to be a true Christian, one must rely directly upon the leading of God's Spirit.

Charismatics contend that spiritual "leading" is manifested in miraculous acts, visions, prophecies, and other supernatural phenomena. Such teachings have the effect of undermining the established authorities and rational procedures of traditional churches. Spontaneous charismatic leadership, devoid of specific qualifications, is made respectable by appeals to the Bible and becomes the source of authority and direction in small groups, prayer cells, and independent churches. Some of these fellowships have developed further into new religious movements; the Children of God and the Northwest Christian community are examples.

---

[19]Wilkerson, with John and Elizabeth Sherrill, *The Cross and the Switchblade* (New York: B. Geis, 1963); Sherrill, *They Speak with Other Tongues* (New York: McGraw-Hill, 1964).

THE SEARCH FOR COMMUNITY

Eschatological and charismatic beliefs have led to the formation of many community-oriented Christian groups. A concern with community is another of the hallmarks of the Abramic tradition. In Judaism and Islam, community is clearly identified with ethnic, national, or religious groups, as Christianity was until the Reformation. Luther's Reformation emphasis on the importance of faith led many Christians to return to a concept of community found in the New Testament, which stresses the idea of the fellowship of true believers sharing a common faith in an essentially hostile and unbelieving world.

The Puritans of the sixteenth century and the Pietists of the seventeenth century are examples of Christian groups that sought to establish new communities of faith. Other outstanding examples of the quest for community include the monastic movements in Roman Catholic, Anglican, Lutheran, and Orthodox traditions and also such groups as the Mennonites, Hutterites, and Doukhobors. Today an emphasis on community has reappeared with new vigor in charismatic circles.

Christian interest in community takes many forms. In the traditional Protestant denominations it has surfaced in revitalization movements that seek to recreate a sense of fellowship among church members. These movements tend to be rational, well controlled, and essentially moderate in beliefs and practices. Within some traditional churches, such as the Roman Catholic and Anglican, charismatic gifts are tolerated and at times even encouraged. They are placed within a framework of tradition and history, however, that tends to encourage respect for rational authority and common sense, thus preventing enthusiasm and cultic practices. The leaders of these mainstream movements tend to be well educated and have considerable theological and biblical knowledge.

By contrast, charismatic groups that emphasize community outside of established denominations tend to arise spontaneously as the result of the conversion experiences of their members. These groups acquire self-appointed leaders who are often poorly educated and theologically unsophisticated. It is out of such groups that many new religions, such as the Children of God, the Local Church, and The Way, have arisen. Both the Children of God and the Local Church place great emphasis on the spiritual nature of leadership. The Way differs from these groups in that its founder was a professor of theology whose search for meaningful community led him to break denominational ties and establish his own group.

PROPHETIC LEADERSHIP

The question of authentic leadership and religious authority is clearly important in judging new religions. Religions of the Yogic tradition revere gurus who gain complete authority over their disciples. Abramic religions have no gurus. Instead, they have the institution of the prophet. A prophet differs from a guru in that the prophet simply declares the Word of God.

Prophets are not held to be gods or to share in the essence of God or even to lead the way to God. They simply serve to remind people of God's Word. Prophets take existing revelation and apply it to particular situations, in the process reminding the people of their failures and calling them to restore their relationship with God. Prophets never develop new doctrines or techniques for attaining salvation. They simply apply existing knowledge and allow their words to be tested against the Scriptures.

Throughout the Bible the testing of prophecy is an important theme. Prophets are called to conform to God's revelation, and the conclusions they draw from particular passages must be fulfilled if their words are to be regarded as authentic. Unlike the guru's teaching, which is tested only by experience, the prophet's teaching is tested by experience, Scripture, and history.

CONCLUSION

Virtually all new religions are largely shaped by the world's two great religious traditions, the Yogic and Abramic. These traditions are very different from one another in their evaluation of human life and destiny. The major difference between new religions and Christianity lies in the fact that all new religions implicitly or explicitly reject Christian teachings about God and human responsibility, denying individual choice and replacing trust in God with magical notions that breed authoritarian organizations and personal dependence.

7

Psychological Aspects of Conversion: The Individual in Crisis

CONVERSION AND THE CULTIC PROCESS

Having learned what myths and traditions new religious beliefs are made of, we should now look at the more personal and social characteristics of people who join cults. We can best do so by taking a closer look at the sort of individual who becomes involved in the cultic process.

The process of creating or looking for and converting to a new religion we call the cultic process. In this and the following chapter, we will look at it in some detail to see what it is that the "seeker" and the new religions do to bring about salvation. The cultic process is fascinating because it forces theologians and social scientists to deal with those subterranean aspects of the individual that we usually prefer to ignore—the phenomena of fragmented beliefs and shattered worldviews. These are characteristically accompanied by anxiety, dread, emotional instability, tension, ennui, and various personal crises.

Personal crises frequently motivate people to search for a meaning system to explain their condition and afford peace; many seek fulfillment within a new social reality. Beyond a meaning system, many also look for a framework of practice in which to express the new meaning. Belief and practice—in short a new lifestyle—enable an individual to engage his or her whole self, so that each movement, each feeling, each thought is reintegrated into a sense of "spiritualized acceptance."

Analytically speaking, the cultic process comprises four major phases. First, a cult or new religion starts when a leader and some close associates externalize and objectify a worldview. They publicize their beliefs, collect followers, and build an organization. Second, individuals experiencing personal crises or generally significant tensions in their environment start to search for a worldview and social setting that will dissolve these tensions and save them and the world from its evils. Third, the searching individuals find the new religion and are socialized into it. Fourth, society generally or those close to these new members (parents, friends, community) react favorably or unfavorably to their commitment and to the new religion. Thus the cultic process includes the combined innovations of the religious entrepreneur, spiritual therapist, lifestyle designer, and, of course, the seeker.

THE INADEQUACY OF OUR CONCEPT OF THE INDIVIDUAL

In our culture, a large number of scholars in the disciplines of religion, philosophy, and the social and physical sciences continue to perceive of men and women primarily as rational beings. As Kenelm Burridge suggests, the dominant anthropological framework still views the human being as a thinker who (1) experiences conflict primarily as mental conflict; (2) becomes aware of this conflict through a process of rationalization, intellectualization, and symbolic representation; and (3) transcends the conflict through a process of rerationalization, antithetical argument, and moral critique.[1]

According to Burridge, the individual is a self that consists of a *person* and an *individual.* By *person* he means the conformist aspect of one's personality that is given to reproducing in word and deed the norms and relations of a given tradition. By *individual* Burridge means that aspect of the self that manifests "relations opposed to those indicated by the person." A self is an individual to the extent that it is a "normal critic who envisages another kind of moral order, the creative spark poised and ready to change tradition." But Burridge contends that this creative spark originates in one's rational faculties.[2]

---

[1]Burridge, *Someone, No One: An Essay on Individuality* (Princeton: Princeton University Press, 1979), p. 7.
[2]Burridge, *Someone, No One,* pp. 5-7.

Peter Berger argues that religion is an "immense projection of human meanings into the empty vastness of the universe—a projection, to be sure, which comes back as an alien reality to haunt its producers."[3] He too considers only the rational aspects of human beings, contending that sociologists of religion must suspend judgment concerning "the question as to whether these projections may not *also* be something else"—which is to say that they must adopt an atheistic methodology. Unfortunately, such an approach projects the rationality of the analyst (the only faculty scientists are supposed to use in their work) onto those being analyzed.

Many social scientists adopt Berger's approach, but in doing so they ignore in themselves and in their analyses important aspects of the human being, aspects that William Barrett has referred to as the "Furies":[4] forces *underneath* intellect and reason. It is precisely this aspect of human nature, these subrational forces, that individuals who search for and join new religions are trying to deal with.

We would do well, then, to start our effort to understand new religions by exploring the perspective of individual *experiences*. Our studies of the life histories of shamans, diviners, "prophets," and members of new religions have led us to the conclusion that the structures of their personal lives are remarkably similar. Our studies indicate that regardless of where these "seekers" or religious practitioners lived—in Africa, Japan, China, Siberia, America, or anywhere else—and regardless of the era in which they lived, they all have very similar life histories. This structural similarity holds up despite differences in idiom, imagery, and cultural contexts. And, significantly, these life histories frequently contradict traditional sociological analyses of both the new religions and their adherents.

We suspect that the constancy in personal lives of these individuals, despite the variety of cultures in which they live and the variety of social scientists who observed them, has something to do with the structure of the human psyche. Beneath the diversity of different cultures, we observe, like Sudhir Kakar, psychological universals.[5]

---

[3]Berger, *The Sacred Canopy: Elements of a Sociology of Religion* (Garden City, N.Y.: Doubleday, 1969), p. 106.

[4]Barrett, *Irrational Man* (Garden City, N.Y.: Doubleday, 1958), pp. 276-79.

[5]Kakar, *The Inner World: A Psycho-analytic Study of Childhood and Society in India,* 2d ed. (New York: Oxford University Press, 1981), p. 10.

It should be noted that there is considerable hostility among members of many new religions to those who want to analyze the psychological state of initiates and more established members. The hostility naturally arises from the fact that analysts tend to attribute the primal experiences of the members exclusively to the biochemistry and psychological make-up of the individuals who have the experiences, whereas members of new religions prefer to attribute them to the existence of a separate spirit world. The former contend that primal experiences are evidence of deviance, whereas the latter contend that they constitute privileged communication.

Ordinary members of new religions have primal experiences quite frequently and in some communities are encouraged to record and circulate them. Leaders of the Unification Church now deemphasize the importance of primal experiences—but they do so not because they have been intimidated by outsiders but because they fear that such experiences might keep members from accomplishing their primary tasks. In a talk entitled "Piety and Spirituality," Unification Church leader Patricia Zulkowsky made this explicit, stating that "such activities are often discouraged since they may distract a person from his mission." In line with an increased emphasis among Unification Church leadership on social action, she concluded by saying that "the restoration of the people in the physical world is most important—as the physical world is restored, the persons in the spirit world will also be restored."[6] Such a conclusion bears strong resemblance to material determinism.

During the discussion accompanying Zulkowsky's talk, however, Thomas McGowan pointed out that of his 74 interviewees, 73 percent reported having had spiritual experiences. Many of them described visionary dreams. In our random interviews of fifteen Unification Church members in Toronto, all but one mentioned spiritual experiences, some of which were quite negative. Two individuals said that they had left the Unification Church for a year or two because they were "spiritually burned out," or had "a breakdown." One sought psychological help outside the Unification Church and later rejoined when he felt "stronger." Yet when McGowan made his observation, Zulkowsky politely dismissed it. "When I said that we de-

---

[6]Zulkowsky, "Piety and Spirituality," lecture delivered at the Bahama Conference, 1980.

emphasized these things," she said, "I meant that our behavior is more important than spiritual experiences."

Unfortunately, many ordinary members do not seem to agree with these leaders. Indeed, Unification Church leaders are becoming adept in the game of intellectual dissimulation. Hallucinations, visionary dreams, and hearing voices are politely called Unification *mysticism*. The fact that "burned out" youths leave the group to recover would seem to suggest that their psychological problems go unnoticed within the Church. What is lacking, of course, is a willingness of Unification Church leaders to reflect seriously upon, and of sympathetic observers to view critically, the obvious discrepancies between reports from ordinary members and leaders.

And yet when a member of the Toronto Unification Church group reported recently that he had had a vision, others in the group were prompted to speak of "the need to move away from intellectualism and to recommit oneself to the *practical* everyday expression of love." One can almost sense the longing for a charismatic revival in this as yet very new charismatic religious movement. It would not be surprising if the day came when some young recruits of the Unification Church split away over the issue of intellectualization versus spirituality. Fortunately for the movement, the young members are kept so busy working that they have little time to reflect seriously about what ails them. In the meantime, and in the name of tolerance, most observers politely refrain from studying the psychological condition of youthful sect members.

VARIATIONS IN NEW RELIGIOUS MOVEMENTS

Different religious groups have different affirmations, renunciations, rituals, core symbols, and dogmas. And just as we stand in judgment of members of new religions, so they stand in judgment of us. At the very least they present a powerful reminder of those human characteristics and behaviors that our scientific theories fail to explain and our mundane, rational world tends to exclude. Nor can we afford to characterize all new religious movements as simply anti-intellectual, anti-modern, or anti-science. What they renounce or affirm are frequently quite subtle shifts in attitude or behavior.

For example, the Rajneesh movement does not renounce wealth. It affirms it. It differs from mainstream society in the means it advocates for acquiring it and the attitude it has toward using it, but on the whole it stands with mainstream society in contrast to more traditional religious attitudes. Consider St. Francis, for instance, who idealized poverty, using nakedness as the master symbol of emancipation from structural and economic bondage. The Rajneeshies hold the color pink, a symbol of spontaneity, freedom, love, and joy, to be the master symbol of emancipation from the seriousness of the world.

Some new religions attempt to unite inner experience with scientific activity. The Unification Church, the Transcendental Meditation movement, and the Rajneeshies all attempt to reunite the subjective with the objective in various ways, achieving various results. They all embrace the fruits of science—technology, medicine, and psychotherapy—but they have different attitudes toward science itself as methodology and a means of explanation. The Rajneesh movement rejects it, the Unification Church seeks a synthesis, and the Transcendental Meditation movement hides its rather traditional religiosity behind it.

Some new religions argue that truth is attained by nonpropositional revelation—that is, by something other than a set of rational propositions. They contend that truth has little to do with ideas but a lot to do with meditation or silence. As the Bhagwan Shree Rajneesh has put it, "Spirituality simply means that you have gone beyond the mind. . . . Ideas as such are transcended."[7] The Reverend Moon favors a more rational approach to truth in his *Divine Principle*.[8]

Similarly, different new religions meet different psychological needs. Some attempt to reorganize a universe that has come crashing down. Others attempt to fertilize and enliven a universe that has become sterile and routine. Some pride themselves in their ability to reduce stress and rebalance a world experienced as "schizoid." Others create schizoid experiences as a way of healing, breaking down the demands of social conformity and bringing new enthusiasm to an unreal situation.

THE PRECULTIC STATE OF THE INDIVIDUAL

Many Americans who join new religions, such as the various Zen groups, come from upper middle class homes in which intellec-

---

[7]Rajneesh, *Guida Spirituale* (Rajneeshpuram, Ore.: Rajneesh Foundation International, 1983), p. 31.

[8]*The Divine Principle* (Washington: Holy Spirit Association for the Unification of World Christianity, 1973).

tual and/or professional achievements are highly valued. The vast majority of such people have had some college education. Their backgrounds are not typically marked by the sort of drastic turmoil found in the ghettos of the cities of the West and throughout the Third World generally.

It is not surprising that the substantial hardships of the Third World produce the sorts of mental confusion and breakdown that lead its victims to search for spiritual healing.[9] It is surprising to discover analogous, if not entirely similar, conditions in wealthier populations. And yet many upper-middle-class youths report that they feel their rational selves have been split from their body, emotions, and the rest of their world. They say that they feel restricted to the rational part of the self, which they refer to as a "coverup," a "lid," or a "theatrical number." They complain that this unreal self conceals either a void or an underlying reality that they view as their true self, which they claim has somehow been lost under the prattle of rationalizations at which people become so adept. The rationalizations have nothing any longer to do with the true self, they say; what there is left of the self is an "act" held together by rational processes that threaten to break down, plunging them into chaos. They say that they have become "hollow forms" devoid of "content."

Many such individuals report that before they entered a new religion their rational thought had become estranged from their physical being, that they no longer experienced thoughts expressed in movements, habits, acts, and feelings. In short, they were troubled by the fact that they felt they had lost *experience* or, more precisely, that they had lost the experience of "thinking and cognition as psychosomatic." A central feature of most new religions is some sort of ritual practice that meets this need to reunify reason with body, mood, and feeling. Many individuals find that such practices allow them to experience life fully in each simple act, in each moment of silence, in being.[10]

---

[9]On this, see Karla Poewe, *The Namibian Herero: A History of Their Psychosocial Disintegration and Survival* (Lewiston, N.Y.: Edwin Mellen Press, 1985).

[10]For a well-documented presentation of the way these people see themselves, see Steven M. Tipton, *Getting Saved from the Sixties: Moral Meaning in Conversion and Cultural Change* (Berkeley and Los Angeles: University of California Press, 1981). Tipton notes that these individuals reported being confronted by a "terrifying" emptiness after "reason was separated from the body," but they also reported that religious rituals transformed the emptiness into "pure awareness" or a blissful state of "nothing" that recreated everything anew. Thus, such rituals fostered a therapeutic form of self-acceptance.

The active estrangement of reason from body to the point that people experience themselves as "false selves" adapted to "false realities" is echoed in the way many members of new religions describe their attitude toward scholarship and the professions prior to joining their particular group. New converts become aware of having sacrificed their notion of the scholar as *seeker* to that of one who merely "kept up" and "did well." Indeed, they are voicing a valid criticism of much modern education. Many academics have forgotten that knowledge is exciting precisely because it identifies and encompasses "real" problems in an experiential world.

Like R. D. Laing in *The Divided Self*,[11] many converts to new religions say that they invert divisions in order to balance them. They say that speech is silence, for instance, and speak of understanding being acted out. Work becomes practice, ritual, or play. Doctrine becomes a practical interpretive framework secondary to the experience of meditation. The individual in relation to "practice" is elevated above the nuclear family. The person becomes the foundation of social life. Interpersonal intimacy is muted to become "transpersonal" intimacy. The future becomes the here and now. The self, once torn by desire and suffering, becomes an unattached and all-accepting consciousness.

SCHIZOID CONDITIONS AND THE SEARCH FOR INTEGRATION

The way of being-in-the-world of those who seek to join new religions is clearly divided. In the discussion that follows, we will be calling it *schizoid*, using Laing's specialized definition: "the term schizoid refers to an individual the totality of whose experience is split in two main ways: in the first place, there is a rent in his relation with his world and, in the second, there is a disruption of his relation with himself. . . . [He] experiences himself as 'split' in various ways perhaps as a mind more or less tenuously linked to a body."[12]

Laing argues that one way of going mad involves a "comprehensible transition from the *sane schizoid* way of being-in-the-world to a psychotic way of being-in-the-world." In his schema, then, *schizoid* and *schizophrenic* are used to refer to sane and psy-

---

[11]Laing, *The Divided Self* (Harmondsworth: Penguin, 1965).
[12]Laing, *The Divided Self*, p. 17.

chotic conditions, respectively. But just as there are ways of going mad, so are there ways of becoming whole. Religious experience is one such way. As Anton T. Boisen has pointed out, certain types of mental disorder and certain types of religious experiences constitute similar attempts at social and psychological *reorganization*.[13] The difference between them lies in the results they produce.

The concept of reorganization is important. We have found that the reorganization of those who join new religions is different from the reorganization of those who do not. Some people experience and/or internalize the world's tensions and *convert;* others experience the same tensions but don't convert.

We have already noted, for example, that prior to conversion, individuals who become members of new religions typically experience a split between reason and emotion—a characteristic that we will subsequently be referring to as *schismogenesis*. Such individuals consequently rely primarily on one faculty or one aspect of their personality, one attitude toward the world, to the detriment of the others. We now wish to suggest that this schismogenesis continues after the individuals join a new religion. The reorganization that they experience does not necessarily—and perhaps never—affect their total personality. Nor is their reorganization merely a matter of a psychological reversal or even a profound spiritual revolution. Their reorganization does not produce a balance, but to the contrary roots them in their imbalance. The imbalanced aspect of their personality is precisely that "single idea" which in "spiritualized" form constitutes the essence of their new religion, and the new religion in turn exacerbates the tendency. Instead of fighting it or repressing it to bring about balance, the new member learns to see it in a new light, to surrender to it and to transform it into pure spirituality.

For example, those who join Buddhist monasteries often note that before they joined, their tendency to rationalize had produced within them a sense of "terrifying emptiness." But now, they say, Buddhist practice has turned this emptiness into "blissful nothing." In the past they repressed or resisted the terror of feeling empty by filling it with words. In the new religion, they no long repress the feeling with rationalizations. Their emptiness has become not just normal, but the very essence of spirituality.

---

[13]Boisen, *The Exploration of the Inner World: A Study of Mental Disorder and Religious Experience* (1936; Philadelphia: University of Pennsylvania Press, 1971).

Instead of resisting it, they are encouraged to surrender to it until they experience it as bliss. The silence that was once hastily covered with words is now bared or even entered into voluntarily through meditation. The major symptom is transformed into the major experience, and their condition is reintegrated into the cosmic order. They feel whole.

Although we can't test it here, it is our hypothesis that those who convert to a (new) religion do so because they can reorganize only with the help of something external. By joining a new religion they regain a sense of balance and well-being at the same time that they come to live in a community of others just like them. They and the new religion constitute their reorganization.

But some people can't convert. While these people feel the world's tensions and go through crises just like those who convert, we suspect that they are able to maintain or reestablish a dynamic balance by themselves with relative ease. It would appear that they experience an intra-individual reorganization. They find that they are able to integrate and even grow with unusual experiences as easily as they can integrate and grow with familiar ones.

As should be apparent, our analysis is significantly different from that of some psychologists and sociologists who are inclined to characterize conversion as a sign of mental illness.[14] Freud and other psychoanalysts have viewed all religious movements as mere projections of neurotic wish-fulfillment or psychotic delusions. We view them as attempts (not always successful) to resolve world and personal disharmony. In this sense, we follow Boisen's lead. He himself was classified schizophrenic and therefore spoke from extreme personal experience as well as objective research. He insisted that the ideas and pictures that flash into the mind as if from an outside source—the "voices" and "visions" that the seeker reports—are not part of a pathology but part of a cure. Within a supportive religious tradition and community, they represent recovery or reorganization. Thus, he contends that primal experiences are psychotherapeutic, not psychopathological phenomena.

Boisen also conducted research while he was a patient in a mental hospital. He found that "many of the more serious psychoses are essentially problem-solving experiences which are closely

---

[14]For a good summary of the psychopathological model of conversion, see William S. Bainbridge and Rodney Stark, *The Future of Religion* (Berkeley and Los Angeles: University of California Press, 1984), pp. 171-77.

related to certain types of religious experience."[15] Indeed, he found that in case after case, individuals would describe the same strange ideas of world catastrophe, death, rebirth, cosmic importance, and mission. The dream content of some Unification Church members has exactly the same structure. And we have found similar phenomena among white Afrikaners in South Africa following the Second Anglo-Boer War (1899-1902) and in the black townships of contemporary Namibia. Poewe refers to people who reported "visions," "psychoses," and the same sense of urgency and mission, some of whom became "prophet-healers" and created independent churches.

Clearly not all those who start or join a new religion will have had upheavals as extreme as that experienced and described by Boisen. Indeed, our model of the cultic process is based on the assumption that the schismogeneses or imbalances most people experience arise from the normal processes in their lives. We might well wonder how many more reports of visions, voices, and other primal experiences there might be if such experiences were not classified as symptoms of insanity in our culture.

THE DEMAND FOR SPIRITUAL EXPLANATION

Schizoid conditions are common. New religions tend to dissolve them into a sense of saving spirituality. Rather than thwarting the drive for self-realization in those who experience a schizoid way of being-in-the-world, new religions bring about a calm self-acceptance.

Not all people who experience their existence as schizoid join new religions. Most find nonreligious ways to deal with their condition. Some receive psychiatric help. Others drift until they reach a state of deterioration that requires hospitalization. Generally, however, people enter a period of searching and find bits and pieces of a new mythology among friends, in literature, drugs, or dharma. They discover, in other words, hints of the possibility of personal wholeness in integral religions.

The psychedelic experience of the sixties introduced a large number of people to a state of consciousness that demanded a spiritual explanation. They found their new awareness to be a mixed blessing, offering not only ecstasy but dread. As Tipton states, "drugs dissolve the relatively rational, reified sense of self maintained by the conscious mind: Drugs take the lid off who you

---

[15]Boisen, *The Exploration of the Inner World*, p. 53.

think you are."[16] Such "uncovering" makes one aware of a formerly concealed underlying reality the exact form of which may well be problematic. As one youth said, "Dope opens you up, for sure, but it also spaces you out."

The psychedelic experience has a significant impact on people. Having surrendered the rational self, they are left with the problem of "how to grasp and reintegrate the nonrational self." The seekers typically search for a way to alter their selfhood. The search often involves an exploration of Eastern philosophy and religions, specifically such ideas as reincarnation, dharma, karma, and yoga. Some seekers visit different cult centers and new religious communities. They participate in feasts, camping weekends, and workshops where they experience new feelings of warmth under the care of devotees. Most eventually find a spiritual home of their own with the group that best meets their need.

OUR THEORY OF CONVERSION TO NEW RELIGIONS

People who shop for alternative religions typically do so because they are experiencing some kind of dissonance and/or schizoid way of being-in-the-world. We have identified two major categories of such schismogenesis—*relational* and *psychological.*

The victims of relational schismogenesis are sometimes said to experience relational double binds. The case of Poppie in Chapter Five (pp. 66-67) provides an example of such a person: a child from a poor working-class background who was sent to a private school where she felt uncomfortable and developed a deep and abiding sense of bitterness. As she became aware that her attitude was costing her friends, she began to search for a solution. When rational and secular solutions didn't work, she began to look for religious solutions. She tried different cults and new religious groups until she found one that accommodated her attitudes, behaviors, and views.

The victims of psychological schismogenesis are sometimes said to experience psychological double binds. Different types of psychological schismogenesis arise from three major and rather separate kinds of discord or conflict. Spiritual schismogenesis arises from a conflict between an inner spiritual world and the external world of reason or unreason and usually leads people to retreat increasingly into a private world of visions, voices, or hallucinations (as in the case of Raymond on pp. 63-66). Rational

---

[16]Tipton, *Getting Saved from the Sixties,* p. 123.

schismogenesis arises from a conflict between reason and emotion (or lost emotion) and usually leads people to engage increasingly in rationalizations that give evidence of their having lost touch with their emotional and physical reality (as in the case of Tim on pp. 67-70). Emotional schismogenesis arises from a conflict between emotion and reality and usually leads people to vent their emotions with increasing frenzy or violence (as in the case of Brian on pp. 70-72). As we will note at greater length in Chapters Nine and Ten, these forms of imbalance are rooted in the common structure of "cultural hysteria" or a "hysterical personality."

Spiritual schismogenesis is often found to occur in people who are physically and/or mentally mistreated early in their lives. The damage is often done prior to age six. Many such individuals are denied parental love and have been raised in foster homes, often having been shuttled from one home to another. This condition is especially prevalent in colored ghettos both in North America and in the Third World, but it is also found among poor whites.

However mild or severe the rejection they suffer, these youngsters learn early to live in an elaborate private world of spirits, voices, visions, vivid dreams, hallucinations, and out-of-body experiences. With increasing age, they may become more bitter and more violent or, alternatively, more withdrawn. Uncomfortable with their personality and lacking a sense of self-esteem, they embark on a spiritual search.

Such primal experiences as visions, coincidences, and revelatory dreams lead individuals to attempt consciously or unconsciously to change their personalities. Primal experiences are usually associated with primal religions and traditional societies. The fact that research indicates their prevalence among white North Americans, Europeans, and people usually classed as schizophrenic substantiates Boisen's point that certain types of mental disorders and certain types of religious experience constitute similar attempts at reorganization. For those suffering spiritual schismogenesis, temporary mental disorders and religious experiences may indicate a healing process.

Rational schismogenesis is the condition that Laing calls "schizoid," and on the whole it entails a less dramatic conflict than spiritual schismogenesis. Victims often come from upper-middle-class or professional homes, and they tend not to feel at home in their own physical body. Typically highly intelligent, they tend to be emotionally clumsy or immature, covering their inadequacy with brash humor, verbal cleverness, or skillful rationalization. These strategies usually serve only to exaggerate their sense of a disrupted relation with their self and the world of more robust individuals around them, however. Uneasy with their emotions and physical being, but aware of somehow having to come to terms with them, such people tend to drift toward new religions that emphasize self-realization through meditation and emotional muting.

Some are made aware of their rational schismogenesis not through psychedelic drugs, meditation, or a religious subculture but by the criticism of other people. Often such individuals feel that others are characterizing them as being physically weak, effeminate, inadequate, or sickly. Sometimes family circumstances necessitate their being raised among a different class of peers—often less intellectual and more physical—and the differences give rise to disparaging comparisons that they cannot deal with easily.

Emotional schismogenesis occurs when people are so overwhelmed by life that they fall apart and sink into emotional chaos. This condition is found frequently in ghettos of the Third World. It occurs less frequently in the West because caretaker professions and institutions tend to prevent extreme emotional confusion or frenzy.

Individuals who find themselves in states of emotional turbulence are rarely able to voice, and still less to analyze, their problems. This makes them susceptible to panic. This condition is common among black women in southern Africa. They are drawn to independent churches that "heal" their condition by ritual massaging, pummeling, shaking, or washing. It is as if "sense" were knocked into them and panic shaken out of them. Once their panic recedes, these women are encouraged to maintain their balance by following further rituals during the course of their daily activities. Holy water is thought to be particularly efficacious.

To sum up, many people who are uncomfortable with their circumstances enter a long search for a religious community in which they can feel at home. In the West, feelings that our world is too impersonal, too rational, and too insincere often give rise to relational, spiritual, and rational schismogeneses—forms of imbalance that are easily accommodated in new religions. In the Third World, on the other hand, material and cultural deprivations and social upheavals often give rise to emotional schismogenesis, a form of imbalance that is typically accommodated by independent faith healing or magical religions.

SCHISMOGENESIS DEFINED

At this point we need to clarify a bit further our conceptualization of the psychological aspects of the cultic process. Schismogenesis, as we are using the term, refers to the complex process of (1) a split in one's relation with the world and oneself; (2) a cumulative, run-away inclination to function within and focus on a single way of being-in-the-world, usually the opposite of the way that is most common among those in one's immediate environment; and (3) an awareness that something is out of balance within oneself. Individuals experiencing schismogenesis characteristically

Table I
Schismogenesis and Cultic Response

Intra-individual schismogeneses	Schismogenetic experience	Reduced social functioning	Methods used by new religions to achieve new harmony
Relational	increasing feeling of bitterness at being socially stigmatized	social withdrawal or physical and political violence	tolerance-learning; discipline-demanding task performance; developing a parental heart
Psychological Spiritual	increasing retreat into an inner world of visions, voices, hallucinations	personal withdrawal, autism, flight	spiritual closing (more food/sleep)
Rational	increasing rationalization belying emotional and physical reality	verbal aggressiveness, flippancy, insensitivity, cynicism, bluffing	silence, meditation
Emotional	increasing emotional frenzy, hysteria, violence	unpredictability and chaotic relations	ritual massaging, washing

perceive this imbalance as "evil" and consider themselves to be in need of "purification." Having come to this conclusion, they usually start looking for ways to "right" themselves.

This definition of the term *schismogenesis* combines ideas of Gregory Bateson and R. D. Laing. Bateson uses the term primarily in reference to systems, however, whereas we use it in reference to individuals. We might also have used such terms as *schizoid, schismodic,* and so forth. We have occasionally used the term *dissonance,* but it has some limiting shortcomings: it seems to imply conflict between two equally strong forces and hence fails to capture the run-away nature of the process that results in an individual's ignoring or flouting social conventions. And this is a key point; we want to stress that it is because individuals are aware that they no longer follow or adhere to the social conventions that they become aware of internal schismogeneses. It is crucial to the process that these individuals *experience* their schismogeneses.

Table 1 shows the four major kinds of intra-individual schismogeneses, indicating how each reduces the individual's ability to function socially and the relevant solutions that different new religions provide. Some upper-middle-class individuals experience no more than a mild form of rational schismogenesis. On the other hand, some less fortunate individuals suffer from several forms of schismogenesis simultaneously. In general, the poor and ghettoized tend to experience more complex emotional schismogeneses.

8

Social Aspects of the Cultic Process: Tensions and Reactions

SOME GENERAL SOCIAL CONTRASTS AND SIMILARITIES

In this chapter we wish to present a broad overview of the cultic process, beginning with some very general observations and then moving to a consideration of more specific social details.

Much of the baby-boom generation will be able to remember the beginnings of the counterculture era in the late 1960s and early 1970s. Young people generally, but especially college students began to experience and express their disillusionment with the politics and warmongering of their elders. We slid into the permissive society. Challenged by the social and cultural confusion of the times, some relationships or marriages broke up, casualties of the tidal wave of sexual permissiveness. And yet most people steered a course somewhere between the conservatism of their parents and the fashionable openness of peers who gave themselves over to drugs, sexual promiscuity, and hippie communities. Most of those who took the middle course then are still doing so today: they did not convert then, and they are not converting now. On the other hand, significant numbers of those who converted to permissiveness then are now converting to new religions.

This crop of converts has some distinctive characteristics. For instance, we have found compelling evidence that the new re-

111

ligions of the 1970s were primarily a middle-class phenomenon, much as the *Bünde* or German Youth Movements were at the turn of the century.[1] Within this group, however, there are some significant differences between converts who come from upper-middle-class backgrounds and converts who come from middle-class backgrounds. These two backgrounds entailed different experiences of affluence, culture, and relationships that affected what young people rejected about society, how secure or insecure they felt concerning their identity, how deeply they sank into the counterculture, and which new religions they tended to join.

Of course the sources of converts for the new religions have changed over time. As movements mature, they tend to change their witnessing techniques. In recent years, for example, the doctrine and goals of the Unification Church have been refined in ways that affect the sorts of people it attracts and the ways it goes about attracting them. What follows is a look into the dynamics of recruitment into new religions during the early counterculture era.

First, we have noted that most of the young people who join ed Buddhist monasteries or the Rajneesh movement during this period came from secure upper-middle-class homes and had parents in the professions or in business. They enjoyed society's privileges. They were expected to enter the professional or business world like their parents, and they were expected to succeed. But they lived in a time of cultural turmoil. Their rational upbringing did not prepare them to deal with the volcanic emotional and spiritual outpourings that were triggered by drugs and much looser, less predictable relationships. They rejected as hypocritical the rationalism of their parents and valued as authentic the spiritual and emotional expressions of the counterculture. When these people joined new religions, it was not so much the prevalence of sexual permissiveness or loose relationships in their society that they were rejecting but the hollowness or emptiness that came with them. They were also rejecting the constraints and tensions associated with their parents' lives.

Being raised in a relatively fluid environment, with considerable choices to make about career and relationship opportunities, produced in many a sense of insecurity about who they were and whether there was a home for them anywhere—and if so, what it would be like. Many became loners, with skills and knowl-

---

[1]See Walter Z. Laqueur, *Young Germany: A History of the German Youth Movement* (London: Routledge & Kegan Paul, 1962).

edge and the liberty to find some kind of job almost anywhere—
or nowhere. They were (and are) perhaps the first generation of
young people in human history who truly belonged to the world.
They were faced with an almost unprecedented obligation to
choose not only careers and partners but also their place in the
world, their home. Predictably, many had difficulty choosing.
They considered themselves misfits, and some were diagnosed as
suffering from personality disorders. A number of individuals
from this group that Bob Mullan interviewed expressed feelings
of rejection and in some cases even paranoia.[2] Uneasy with themselves as social isolates, many entered a path of psychotherapy
through reading, drugs, occult groups, therapy cults, left-wing
political groups, and so on. It would appear that they turned to
such methods in order to strengthen the self, which they perceived to be the primary means by which they would be able to
succeed in life.

The young people from this group who entered Buddhist
monasteries learned to lead simple spiritual lives. They were
taught to mute their emotional expressiveness, but they received
no proscriptions of sexual permissiveness (at least in the sense
that the American Buddhist sexual ethic is not based on
exclusivity). They were taught that close interpersonal ties or ties
based on intimacy are unimportant. Emphasis was placed on
transpersonal ties, which is to say that they were introduced to a
solitary sociality as opposed to a pattern of relationships based on
couples or nuclear families.

Rajneeshies, who have since left Oregon, differ from American Buddhists in their emphasis on open expression of exaltation,
joy, and emotional euphoria. They not only allow sexual permissiveness but advocate it. According to the Bhagwan Shree
Rajneesh, sex is not merely a personal indulgence but a "vehicle
for the highest freedom." It must be enjoyed until for the man,
"the whole universe has become woman," and for the woman,
"the whole universe has become man." In "The Tantra of Erotic
Love," Rajneesh admonishes that "unless you are overflowing
with your own bliss, you are a danger to society, because a person
who sacrifices always becomes a sadist."[3] Seekers who are not interested in sex, he says, are in fact not seekers at all. Rajneeshies
proudly claim that their community is free of tension and stress.

---

[2]See Mullan, *Life as Laughter* (London: Routledge & Kegan Paul, 1983).
[3]Rajneesh, "The Tantra of Erotic Love," *Resurgence* 5 (May-June 1974):
11-16.

This claim is belied, however, by the factionalism and breakup of Rajneeshpuram in 1985.

The Rajneeshies are like American Buddhists in propounding and practicing a transpersonal sociality. If they do not totally reject the nuclear family, they believe that it is clearly less desirable than solitary sociality. But again, although the sociality of the two groups is similar, the American Buddhists practice a quiet blissfulness through meditation, whereas the Rajneeshies practice an expressive blissfulness through emotional arousal.

People who have joined the Unification Church or Hare Krishna communes have mostly come from nonprofessional middle-class homes, although the overall socio-economic background of members of the Unification Church ranges across a wide spectrum that includes some upper-middle, lower-middle, and even working-class people. Those who joined Hare Krishna during the 1960s tended to come from affluent but non-professional middle-class homes (in which fathers were well-paid truck drivers and the like). Thus, they had typically enjoyed money and material comforts but remained, in a sense, culturally deprived. Many such individuals participated in student demonstrations and protests in the 1960s, and many came to the conclusion that their parents' faith was patently hypocritical and offered no key to meaning in life. Furthermore, most of those who joined Hare Krishna had first been hippies in the 1960s.

A key point distinguishing those who joined the Unification Church and Hare Krishna from those who joined the American Buddhists and Rajneeshies is their firm rejection of the permissive society and especially sexual promiscuity. They maintained that the jealousy and uncertainty that came with the loosening of man-woman ties was too great a price to pay for sexual freedom. They rejected the values of fluidity and tentativeness, harkening back to the values of faith, chastity, asceticism, commitment, good social conduct and, if not poverty, then at least simplicity. Spiritual and emotional highs were emphasized (although they are now being deemphasized in the Unification Church). In effect, these two groups are echoing the medieval vows of poverty, chastity, and obedience.

The Unification Church clearly placed more emphasis on spirituality at its inception, but it has increasingly made social action—specifically, world restoration—its primary goal. Accompanying its proscription of permissiveness is an emphasis on interpersonal rather than solitary sociality; the nuclear family is central to its dogma. The Church has mounted international social projects, drawing on the services of scholars and theologians through conferences and various organizations. The degree of theological sophistication and self-discipline among the Church's leaders continues to increase, creating a widening gap between them and the Church's laity. Leaders genuinely live the Principle, successfully integrating their theology with their behavior, but on the whole the members are not similarly successful.

Members of Hare Krishna, like those of the Unification Church, practice an interpersonal sociality that is more or less as ascetic. Unlike members of the Unification Church, however, they do not seek to transform the world but rather to transform themselves and to bring about a change of heart in the world's people. Once individuals join the movement, they continue to experience the mysticism and spiritualism that they experienced before they joined. Nevertheless, it is based on chanting of the mantra and the consumption of vegetarian diets rather than on taking drugs as was the case for many during their days as hippie.[4]

Restorative or reformative movements such as the Unification Church and utopian movements such as the Rajneeshies tend to be interethnic and international in orientation (although the Rajneesh movement is much more exclusive than the Unification Church—the criterion of exclusivity being not ethnic or national origins but wealth and skills). By contrast, conversionist movements such as the Hare Krishna and introversionist movements such as American Zen Buddhists contain primarily white upper-middle-class members.

To summarize some major distinctions, we would note again that the Unification Church and Hare Krishna, though communal, practice an interpersonal sociality and an asceticism in reaction to societal permissiveness. American Buddhists and Rajneeshies, also communal, practice a transpersonal sociality and in a sense push societal permissiveness to its utopian limits. The Rajneeshies go so far as to suggest that sexuality is the means to a greater spirituality.

Of these four movements, the Unification Church is neoconservative. Its explicit goal is world restoration. The other

---

[4]See Jeanne Francine Danner, *The American Children of Krsna* (New York: Holt, Rinehart & Winston, 1976), and J. Stilson Judah, *Hare Krishna and the Counter Culture* (London: John Wiley, 1974).

three movements are romantic and have variously conservative and liberal aspects. Their goals are self-actualization by way of tidbits of exotic rituals and wisdom. While all movements initially rejected intellectualism and embraced emotional or spiritual euphoria, the Unification Church now is emphasizing the importance of intellectually or ideologically informed behavior and is deemphasizing spirituality.

With the possible exception of the Unification Church and the American Zen Monasteries, one suspects that most of these groups will be single-generation phenomena. They may succeed in reminding us that such institutions as our families, our churches, and our educational institutions are in danger of becoming hollow because they are crowding out emotion, spirit, spontaneity, and experience in their single-mindedly rational and science-based approach to life. We can only hope, however, that members of these groups will in turn relearn from us that there is no quick and easy way to salvation. A spiritual high, no matter how frequently repeated, cannot take the place of systematic, cumulative learning.

SOCIOLOGICAL DISAGREEMENTS

We have noted the importance of family and socio-economic background as a factor among those who joined new religions. Before we move on, we should take note once more of four other key factors involved in the emergence of new religions during the 1970s: (1) the general and swift socio-cultural changes of the sixties and the confusion they produced; (2) the specific geographical region, especially California, in which many of the new churches first emerged; (3) the fact that these religious movements are a middle-class phenomenon, especially among would-be and/or disillusioned intellectuals; and (4) the fact that all new religions have either exotic-romantic or neo-conservative tendencies. While the movements in Germany and Austria at the turn of the century hearkened back to medieval times and ways, some new movements of our era hearken back to earlier times of other cultures.

Three major positions concerning the meaning of new religions for Western society and the established churches have emerged during the past decade. One is outlined by Bryan Wilson in his book *Contemporary Transformations of Religion*, another is outlined by William S. Bainbridge and Rodney Stark in *The Fu-*

ture of Religion, and a third is outlined by Steven Tipton in *Getting Saved from the Sixties.*[5]

Wilson argues that the process of secularization is irreversible. He maintains that all evidence points to the "decline of belief in the supernatural, and the rejection of the idea that the supernatural has any significant influence in the everyday life of modern man." Not only has belief in the supernatural decreased, but human beings now seem "strongly convinced that religion has diminishing importance in the social order."[6] Wilson cites a number of "transformations" of religion that confirm the trend he describes, indicating the extent to which religion has become inconsequential for modern society.

By contrast, Bainbridge and Stark, along with Roy Wallis and others, argue that the new religions are filling a vacuum left by the decline of the Roman Catholic Church and the mainline Protestant churches. Bainbridge and Stark use a market model to explain the losses and gains of old and new religions, maintaining that new religions constitute an expression of religious revival.

Tipton is more concerned with the kinds and meanings of religious transformations than he is with the issue of secularization. He agrees with Wilson that the influence of religion on American life has declined, diminishing especially in the period from 1965 to 1975, but he notes that it has rebounded somewhat since then, to the point that it now exerts about half the influence it did in the mid-1950s. He argues that the decline in the influence of religion on American life coincided with the decline in influence of fundamentalist biblical morality, with its emphasis on authority and obedience. More importantly, it also coincided with the decline in influence of the utilitarian ethic, which prizes above all the efficient accumulation of wealth and power.

The turmoil of the 1960s generated the expressive ethics of the counterculture, at the heart of which is a nontheistic conception of divinity and the fundamental assumption of an acosmic monism, the notion that all is one, that everything is essentially

---

[5]Wilson, *Contemporary Transformations of Religion* (London: Oxford University Press, 1976); Bainbridge and Stark, *The Future of Religion: Secularization, Revival and Cult Formation* (Berkeley and Los Angeles: University of California Press, 1984); and Tipton, *Getting Saved from the Sixties: Moral Meaning in Conversion and Cultural Change* (Berkeley and Los Angeles: University of California Press, 1981).

[6]Wilson, *Contemporary Transformations of Religion,* p. 15.

pure energy or existence without any enduring structure or logos. It is an ethic of "love"—the sort of universal love and respect for life that goes hand in hand with the assumption that all life is united and all existence is one.

Counterculture ideology holds that human beings are basically good and that one need only be self-aware and self-expressive to bring about good consequences. Moreover, if one is good, then it is also safe to "do one's own thing," to "let it all hang out," to live only in the here and now, and to rely on one's intuition and feelings about a situation. External restraint is unnecessary because the actions of good people won't harm anyone. People needn't *do* things with one another to express the best that is in them; they need merely *be* with each other.

This countercultural myth is found among the Rajneeshies today in their concept of fusion or *mystical merger*. In the sixties it was enacted in psychedelic, musical, sexual, and meditative experiences in which individuals felt the self merging and becoming one with others and all existence. Most contemporary new religions continue to emphasize one or several of these experiences within communal contexts.

Monism and self-expressiveness result in sensitivity toward self and others, and communities that prize these values are characteristically held together by individual self-expression. The social structure of such communities is usually egalitarian. Where leaders emerge, their authority is based not on bureaucratic office or traditional station but on exemplary charisma. Followers respond to the manifestation of the leader's extraordinary personality. In short, the leaders exemplify the movement's primary goals: self-awareness, self-expression, and self-realization. All of this means that the goal and means are one and the same in this scheme of things. The end or future is therefore in the present.

In any case, such was the blissful vision of the counterculture at a time of secure affluence, when the virtues of suffering and pain looked nonsensical. But the sixties ended. Youths became young adults and found themselves in competition for scarce jobs and positions. It was during this phase in their lives, just as they were making the transition into adulthood, that most young people experienced the conflicts of opposite cultural values in a particularly profound way. "Disoriented by drugs, embittered by politics, disillusioned by the apparent worthlessness of work and the transiency of love, they have found a way back through" new religious movements, says Tipton, "a way to get

along with conventional American society and to cope with the
demands of their own maturing lives."[7]

Where Tipton differs from both Wilson's skepticism and
Bainbridge and Stark's optimism, then, is in his belief that new religions are *mediative successors* to the conflicts of the 1960s: they
mediate between the old biblical and utilitarian ethics and the
new expressive morality. He argues that new religions synthesize
valuable elements of the counterculture with the most function-
ally necessary conditions of modern society.

While we basically agree with Tipton, we are a little less optimistic about the intent and ability of new religions to synthesize
the ethic of the counterculture with that of the established mainline culture. The notion of synthesis of conflicting opposites is too
simple to account for cultic reality. Dialectical syntheses are on
the whole a good deal easier to hypothesize than to find worked
out in the real world. Such synthesis as is evident among the new
religions is found primarily in the neoconservative Unification
Church, but even here it is overshadowed by a growing gap between the leaders, who are trying to make the Church acceptable
to society by intellectualizing its doctrine and rationalizing its
structure, and the followers, who continue to expect and yearn
for an expressive lifestyle based on equality, self-realization, and
spontaneity.

Rather than mediate anything, it seems to us that most new
religions prolong the counterculture experience and, for that
matter, the trappings of youth. In well-funded communes, members of new religions can "drop out" and "tune in" more seriously
and systematically than before. At least that is what the practices
of Rajneeshies, Hare Krishnas, and Zen Buddhists would lead us
to believe.

Unless members of new religions accept the fact that experiential knowledge can no more than complement rational knowledge, mediation and synthesis are out of the question and their
new religions will fall silent like their gurus, to become, at most,
splendid failures. Alternatively, they may revert to rationalization
and institutionalization and become businesses that sell therapies. Finally, some may become established churches that differ
relatively little from what we have now, except that their organization may more systematically resemble large international
corporations.

---

[7]Tipton, *Getting Saved from the Sixties*, p. 15.

FROM INTERPERSONAL TO TRANSPERSONAL TIES

At this juncture we should recap a few points made earlier: (1) some new religions emphasize *transpersonal* rather than interpersonal ties; (2) individuals who join these sorts of new religions usually come from upper-middle-class and/or professional homes; and (3) the schismogenetic experiences these individuals have are most often of the rational and relational type.

Affluent seekers are characteristically disillusioned with wealth first because they have found that it does not automatically provide emotional or spiritual fulfillment and second because they have found that it shatters belief in the sanctity of interpersonal ties, usually starting with the ties between lovers or spouses. The affluent tend to experience an isolation that comes with a life of relative ease and fluid relationships. Theirs is not the isolation of suburban housewives, trapped and frustrated within the confines of the modern nuclear family. Theirs is an isolation amid comforts. It is their tragedy that their lives appear to be free of tragedy. As members of a mobile middle class, they are supposed to be above suffering, above pain, above being shattered. But such expectations are themselves shattered under the pressures of reality, and the result, in some cases, is rational schismogenesis, a feeling that one's emotions have been divorced from one's rational self.

As we have noted, a large number of these affluent seekers turn to utopian and introversionist movements such as the Rajneeshies and the American Buddhists. In interviews, Rajneeshies speak of having obtained relief from the pressures of their precultic lives in the alternating bouts of silence, crying, and laughter that they experienced during their transition to Rajneeshism.[8] Most of these individuals appear to have been quite aware of their profound identity disturbances before joining the Rajneeshies. Indeed, there is evidence that many of them made valiant efforts through much of their lives to correct or master their personality disorders—an indication of courage, not narcissism.

Burdened with a sense of the shallowness and flightiness of human ties, especially romantic ties, affluent seekers (perhaps to their credit) reject conservative belief in marriage for the sake of establishing a family and turn instead to communities in which

---

[8]See Mullan, *Life as Laughter*, pp. 50-79.

their experience of shallow interpersonal ties is affirmed but given a new positive meaning.

The lack of mutual commitment between man and woman or, what amounts to the same thing, the easy access to new partners for temporary and rather shallow relationships, is the latest crisis in the lifestyle of successful singles—a situation that has led even formerly militant feminists to advocate a more conservative approach to relationships. In her recent book *Sex and Destiny*, for instance, Germaine Greer advocates a return to coitus interruptus or celibacy.[9] Others urge a return to traditional marriages and family life. The crisis in the American family that has led to such changes in outlook is one of several factors that has led to looser interpersonal ties between spouses. The tie between husband and wife has always been weaker than the tie between parent and child in American families, but recently it has been weakening even further—as witness the unprecedented divorce statistics.

In most American families the strength of the ties between husband and wife deteriorates relatively quickly, often detectably within the first year of marriage. What keeps many marriages from breaking up is the arrival—sometimes calculated, sometimes not—of children. The tasks of raising children and earning salaries become more important preoccupations for husband and wife than their interpersonal ties, and the demands that both place on their relationship typically diminish.

Walter Trobisch has pointed out that the Christian vision of marriage amounts to more than the typical American version. Significantly, he clarifies the meaning of marriage—becoming "one flesh"—in the African context. Following a long discussion about marriage with his African congregation, he asked them "What is the last thing in this verse of Genesis 2:24?"

"It's the word *flesh*," an elderly man answered.

"No," said Trobisch. "What comes after *flesh*?"

There was a long silence. Finally, a young man said, "A full stop."

Then Trobisch went back into the pulpit and read the Bible verse again: "Therefore a man leaves his father and his mother and cleaves to his wife, and they became one flesh." Striking his fist on the lectern, he added, "Full stop."[10]

The following day Trobisch explained to his congregation

---

[9]Greer, *Sex and Destiny* (London: Secker & Warburg, 1984).
[10]Trobisch, *I Married You* (New York: Harper & Row, 1971), p. 20.

that God blessed Adam and Eve and only then told them to "be fruitful and multiply." It was, he emphasized, an *additional* action. And so, he said, "when the Bible describes the indispensable elements of marriage, it is significant that children are not expressly mentioned. Leaving, cleaving, and becoming one flesh are sufficient. Full stop."

In America, however, the idea of "one flesh" has on the whole lost its meaning, if indeed it ever had any. It is only conjured up by a resistant spouse threatened with an unwanted divorce.

The loss of this sacred notion of marriage is symptomatic of a more general abandonment of the idea that committed interpersonal ties are possible. And for the people who have abandoned this idea, the Rajneesh movement offers consolation: it allows the affluent to enjoy their affluence free of guilt, free of emotional or spiritual deprivation, and—importantly—free of the illusion that meaningful interpersonal ties are possible. Their main schismogenetic experience is affirmed as correct by the movement.

The Rajneeshies free their members of guilt about their affluence by having all of them participate in doing menial work. They free their members of emotional and spiritual deprivation by offering practices that induce euphoria. They free their members of nagging longings for unrealizable interpersonal ties by generating spiritual commitment to the Bhagwan and social commitment to the community. This commitment to the community is not a matter of concrete social relationships or relationship networks but of a common acceptance of one spiritual authority who dispenses euphoria in which all share.

In the final analysis, however, it is ironic that the affluent should opt for a totalitarian religion and lifestyle. Whatever criticisms they may have of the affluent society, their totalitarian solution would be disastrous if instituted in our society as a whole. Like the fascism that gained popularity among the poor and defeated in the thirties, this religious totalitarianism may serve to point out much that is negative in our social life. In itself it is not a viable alternative social doctrine or system.

RELIGIOUS TRANSFORMATIONS AND THEIR IMPACT ON SOCIETY

In order to understand the transformations of new religions, we would do well to compare what the churches of the 1800s fought for and against with what new religions fight for and against today.

As bourgeois capitalism and Marxist socialism grew in Europe in the nineteenth century, so did Christian criticism of the mechanical and economic concepts of society. Many Christians were opposed to the mechanistic conception of society and fought for the integration of industrial structures into a nonmechanical social order.

As we have noted, new religions that adopt Eastern practices assume an acosmic monism: "all is one." Instead of emphasizing the ethnic and racial differences in the human community that obligate us to be tolerant toward others, such new religions emphasize their vision of the essential oneness of man. Their devotees try above all to maintain a sense of equilibrium and to avoid strife. They work to understand the meaningfulness of our oneness. Such attitudes offer an implicit criticism of our pluralistic social order and of society based on social programs and vested interests.

Some of the young people who join new religions reject the bureaucratic and rationalistic concept of society. Societies of this sort require people to play multiple roles in order to achieve rational integration into various institutions, and they contend that role playing makes people lose touch with their sense of self, renders them inauthentic, and alienates them from their feelings.

Back in the 1800s, Quaker industrialists sought to restore the humanity of their employees by advocating decent working conditions, a living wage, and protection against accidents. In taking such actions they were not merely trying to improve the workers' physical lot but also to restore their humanity, to acknowledge their individuality and personality apart from their machinelike existence in the social order. They saw the need to stop treating people like numbers, to give them back some self-respect, and to affirm their intellectual and moral independence.

Upper-middle-class young people today perceive a different sort of problem. They are not so much concerned with people-as-numbers as with people-as-roleplayers. They are not so much concerned with restoring independence as with restoring a sense of wholeness, which they generally define in terms of self-awareness and self-expressiveness. They already have intellectual and moral independence, but they still do not know who they are. Too often they feel themselves to be someone's concept of what they should be—typically their parents' concept. They want freedom from concepts and freedom from learned patterns. Zen-based new religions teach these individals (and remind us all) that there is merit in achieving an awareness of self in each moment and place.

In the 1800s Christians fought to maintain the free personality and the rational existence of the individual by offering their children a nonmechanist and noneconomic concept of humanity. Today devotees of some new religions fight to maintain human spontaneity and the holistic existence of the individual by offering the devotee a nonanalytical and nonrationalistic sense of humanity. European Christians of the 1800s attempted to replace Economic Man with a Christian vision; adherents of many new religions attempt to replace all unidimensional conceptions of human nature with a nontheistic spiritual concept.

Another point of difference between Christians and members of Eastern-influenced cults is that the former characteristically seek to endure the present and live for the future, whereas the latter typically seek to experience simple pleasures fully and without guilt in the here and now. Members of such cults stress awareness of the immediate situation rather than knowledge of a coming apocalypse.

The danger for Christians and Christian sectarians has always been their insistence that they know and own the Truth, their inclination to take things that are culturally relative and insist that they are religious absolutes. Young people raised in an international and interethnic world instinctively reject such conceit. They are inclined not so much to assert Truth as to attempt to understand and explore their own mind and feelings. Suspicious of liberal hypocrisy, they try to understand reality by getting in touch with the awareness through which one knows rather than settling for only what the mind knows. A key feature of this awareness of thoughts, feelings, and emotions that they are seeking is experience of the root source of those thoughts, feelings, and emotions. For those who say they are not prejudiced and yet feel and act prejudicially, learning to become aware of the root source of their feelings would be liberating. It might not turn them into totally new people, but it could teach them humility and honesty.

New religious movements are highly individualistic, stressing either the individual self or the self-selected community. Bryan Wilson has pointed out a number of the negative social consequences of such new religions. "They promise, whether by regimen of asceticism or by a license for hedonism, or by a mixture of the two, to increase the happiness and the spiritual power of their devotees in this world and to protect them from the limitations and dangers of everyday life," he says. They all offer "new freedom, new power, new sense of peace that can be obtained quickly and relatively easily" but they do not offer the sorts of eternal truths that can be handed down from father to son.[11] They are transient faiths, he argues, offering salvation through self-realization or through a sacred community and using strange and exotic symbols to titillate jaded sensibilities rather than teaching sustained knowledge. At most such religions simply make personal ecstasy routine rather than transforming it into a lifetime of grace as religions have sought to do in the past.

Wilson's criticism is well taken. His point that new religious movements are highly individualistic is quite correct. But it is a valid question whether post-Enlightenment Christianity has provided us with any better social solutions. Peter F. Drucker has argued that those who have sought social purpose in Christianity have been unable to find any in it, that they have had to settle for individualistic faith.[12]

Reviewing the thought and work of famous Christian thinkers and activists, Drucker underscores the importance of Christianity for the individual. Dostoevski came to the conclusion that only individual Christians can make the modern world rational and sensible so that it can endure its reality. Henry Adams reacted against the demonic nature of the machine in modern society and searched for the "full life" in which people could live in an united, sensible order. But in the end he too decided that he could derive only individual values from religion. Kierkegaard fled to God once he recognized that the individual is but an isolated atom in the modern world. But all he could find in Christianity was the strength to make loneliness tolerable and sensible. Chesterton worked for a social rather than a private religion, but, says Drucker, the only social ideal he produced was *The Return of Don Quixote*—"the most asocial, most isolated figure in all literature who lives entirely in his own personal imagination" and overlooks all social reality.[13]

Drucker concludes that the most these great Christians could find in their faith to offer others was "a private haven and

---

[11]Wilson, *Contemporary Transformations of Religion*, p. 62.
[12]Drucker, *The End of Economic Man* (New York: John Day, 1939), pp. 101-3.
[13]Drucker, *The End of Economic Man*, p. 101.

refuge in an individual religion. They cannot give a new society and a new community." He suggests that the "clearest and most pathetic example of the social failure of Christianity" is that of the brave and valiant leader of the German confessional movement Martin Niemöller. Niemöller had been a submarine commander during the First World War and came out of it a crushed and uprooted man. He searched for a new society among the socialist and communist workers and even among the first radical Nazi groups. "Finally, he turned toward religion. He found in religion an individual peace and an individual haven, an individual mission and an individual faith. But he did not find in it a lesson for society."[14]

In general, then, modern Christianity has tended either to retreat into individual piety or adopt a plan of social activism that entails abandoning traditional piety (as in the case of Third World liberation theologies). The only modern exception to the tendency of Christians to follow one or the other of these paths is the Dutch neo-Calvinist movement that developed during the nineteenth century under the leadership of Abraham Kuyper.[15] But, apart from this movement, which was at once pious and socially influential, neither mainstream Christian groups nor quasi-Christian new religions have developed social or political creeds that correspond to their personal religion. Perhaps it is not—at least not since the Middle Ages—the function of religions to do so. If so, we have all the more reason to look closely at what new religions are telling us about the state and needs of the individual.

We have already noted that modern new religions are highly influenced by religious practices that come to us from the East and the Third World. There is a general perception among those who join these new religions that they offer the sort of personal experience, spirituality, and emotion that are no longer available in conventional religious institutions. It is as if the emphasis on organizational structure, doctrinal formality, intolerance of contradictions and inconsistencies in ideology or theology in the Christian churches have aged them and rendered them sterile. The religiosity of less-developed countries is less subject to these deadening demands of rationality. Their religions continue to emphasize symbolic representation, emotional expression, inspirational receptiveness, and assurance or solace.

[14]Drucker, *The End of Economic Man*, p. 102.
[15]See McKendree R. Langley, *The Practice of Political Spirituality: Episodes from the Public Career of Abraham Kuyper, 1879-1918* (Jordan Station, Ont.: Paideia Press, 1984).

The Western world has long exported rationality and the concept of individual rights to the rest of the world. More recently, we have begun to import religious revitalization movements from the developing world, including euphoric rituals and intense allegiance to charismatic leaders. Indeed, Wilson has suggested that intense allegiance to charismatic leaders, sets of rites, and prophecies constitute functional substitutes for intense belief in an exclusive body of doctrine.[16]

It is simply a psychological fact that *intense* allegiance is typically associated with the sorts of experiential phenomena in the life of an individual that our Western science and education ignore.

We should also be alert to the fact that religious revitalization movements imported from less developed countries that are torn by political divisions, social disintegration, armed conflict, and religious diversity (e.g., Korea and South Africa) will often contain elements of a vision of a new and better world. It is important that we consider the political and social implications of the social mythologies of these new religions for our own society. As Anthony Wallace has pointed out, we need to study not just how a prophet's visionary reformulation of reality is communicated and transformed into an organization but also how it is adapted to different individual and societal needs and whether it is able to revitalize these.[17]

In a new social setting, the sort of cultural transformation that an imported new religion ostensibly champions may be altered as the new religion shifts its interests to such matters as simple survival, the preservation of doctrine, and the performance of ritual. In the case of the Unification Church, for instance, efforts to ensure survival diverted the body from the program of social reform it had initially intended to usher in.

SOCIAL ASPECTS OF NEW RELIGIONS: A SUMMING UP

In his classic study *Religious Sects*, Bryan Wilson defines sects as "movements of religious protest" and distinguishes seven different types: conversionist, revolutionist, introversionist, manipulationist, reformist, utopian, and thaumaturgical.[18] Those wishing

---

[16]Wilson, *Magic and the Millennium* (New York: Harper & Row, 1973).
[17]Wallace, "Revitalization Movements," *American Anthropologist* 58 (1956).
[18]Wilson, *Religion Sects* (New York: McGraw-Hill, 1970), pp. 7, 38-40.

more information on these categories should consult his extensive discussion both in *Religious Sects* and in *Magic and the Millennium*. Evidence we have gathered indicates that the sects that
have arisen during the past few decades also fit into this scheme.
In that connection we would like to explore the external conditions in which different types of sects tend to develop and
the social impact, if any, that sects have on their surrounding
environment.

While *conversionist* sects may recur in any pioneer setting
and under any conditions of social upheaval or social dislocation,
other sects occur in more restricted circumstances or take on re-
strictive attitudes in widely different environments.

Revolutionist sects are rare in today's world, having peaked
in the Third World during the period of cultural confusion and social upheaval that followed initial contact with the West. Anthropologists described many of these revitalization or nativistic
movements in Oceania, Africa, and among Native Americans at
the turn of the century and as recently as the 1960s. Revolutionist
sects were typified by expectations of an apocalypse and the coming of a new world, but members of such sects usually did not expect that they would play a vital role in this upheaval. At most,
they attempted to hurry in the cataclysm by destroying their
wealth and then waiting for God to usher in the new age.

Thaumaturgical sects are also found principally in the Third
World, but unlike revolutionist sects, many of them are still vital-
ly active today. Independent churches of South Africa present
perhaps one of the most dramatic examples of such sects. They
seek to bring personal and local salvation through the healing of
physical and mental suffering and illness. The emphasis is on
bringing about relief from present ills, tensions, and discomforts.
In this, they resemble manipulationist sects to some extent, although manipulationist sects typically offer shortcuts to prestige
and power, whereas thaumaturgical sects typically seek to restore the sorts of capacities to individuals who have "fallen apart"
that will allow them to function in society.

The "prophets" of these thaumaturgical sects assume that
psychogenic and other mental disturbances, purely organic disorders, and misfortunes generally all have their roots in interpersonal and social conflicts. Such conflicts create tensions, fears,
anxieties, hysteria, and related psychoneuroses as well as headaches, intestinal problems, and other aches and pains that the
prophets are generally able to sort out and treat effectively. The
subjects that these prophets treat tend (1) to be dependent and

conforming in character, (2) to have lost hope or become generally submissive, (3) to have suppressed normal self-assertive tendencies and therefore become dependent on ingratiation or manipulation, and (4) to have suffered from a deep conviction of defeat and insignificance since early childhood.

Manipulationist sects have as their goal a this-worldly salvation through success that is to be attained by improving especially the mind. These sects are neither familial nor communal; rather, they are highly individualistic, defining the identity of the adherent in terms of his or her success in the competitive struggle of everyday life. Manipulationist sects offer objective achievement and psychic reassurance. Emphasis is placed on mental hygiene. While some still subscribe to a physical regimen, mostly these sects leave the physical care of the body to physicians. The West is riddled with groups of this kind—Transcendental Meditation, EST, Theosophy, Christian Science, Scientology, and so on.

Manipulationist sects arise in settings in which people have become highly individuated and are strongly oriented to personal achievement. Wilson contends that they flourish in societies with considerable job and professional diversification and that they attract that segment of the population that is semi-sophisticated in their ability to imitate the genuine reasoning of philosophers and scientists. Manipulationist sects are universalist and urban oriented. Members clearly value worldly well-being. They are articulate and eager for shortcuts to prestige and power. Older manipulationist sects, which were concerned primarily with physical health, tended to attract especially middle-aged urban women. Today these sects emphasize expansion of consciousness and mental health and attract younger, upwardly mobile sections of the population.

Introversionist sects also tend to attract more sophisticated segments of populations. Because they tend to reject dominant moral and religious attitudes, however, they are rarer in Western societies. Introversionist sects assume that the world is evil and they seek salvation through withdrawal from it and a cultivation of personal holiness. American Zen Buddhism and the Hare Krishna movement are both introversionist sects (although some Zen centers are becoming somewhat reformist in orientation). Such sects can survive only in societies that tolerate a good deal of social and ideological diversity. Laws enforcing compulsive education, health and sanitation regulations, taxation, military service, and so on tend to make them a rarity even in modern pluralistic societies. Importantly, these sects circumvent educa-

tional and other problems by deemphasizing family and offspring. The Hare Krishna movement, which does value the family
and children, is only beginning to grapple with the problem of education.

We have already said a good deal about *reformist* movement, such as the Unification Church, and *utopian* movements,
such as the Rajneeshies. In the modern Western context,
reformist movements tend to be neoconservative in tone; utopian
movements tend to be neoromantic. The goal of reformist movements is to overcome the world's evils through reform in accord-
ance with the dictates of conscience. Utopian sects search for salvation through radical reconstruction based on eclectic religious
principles, seeking to build a little world of their own without tension, a world of joy, a world that can eventually be opened to include everyone.

In conclusion, three points are worth repeating. First, religious movements or sects may change from one type to another
during the course of their history. Second, only revolutionist and
reformist sects tend to have social impacts. Most movements enhance individual growth, healing, self-expression, or self-
actualization. In that sense they cater to the unrooted, if not uprooted, middle class. Third, while reformist movements,
especially following successful adaptation to the larger society,
tend to accommodate individuals with any of the four
schismogenetic disturbances, other movements are more restric-
tive. Here too we must remember, however, that the attraction of
specific sectors of the population or category of persons has
much to do with a movement's historical development. It appears
that individuals suffering spiritual schismogenesis will be most
attracted to conversionist and revolutionist sects in their early
stages. Individuals suffering rational schismogenesis will be most
attracted to introversionist and manipulationist sects in their
early stages. Individuals suffering relational schismogenesis will
be most attracted to reformist and utopian movements. And individuals suffering emotional schismogenesis will be most attracted to thaumaturgical sects. The more institutionalized a sect becomes, however, the more attractive it becomes to a wider
spectrum of people.

9

The Psychology of Shamanism: Some Cross-Cultural Comparisons

In previous chapters, we have noted that the religious practices of non-Western cultures have found their way into new religions in North America. Moreover, we have suggested that a common psychology underlies all of these therapeutically effective religions. We find this commonality in the similar primal experiences of converts to all manner of different religions in different places and times, as well as in their life histories and personalities.[1] In this and the next chapter we will bring these ideas together by addressing three major issues. First, we want to take a closer look at the nature of non-Western *shamanistic* religions. Second, we want to consider the nature and role of primal experiences in shamanistic religions as well as in our imported new religions. And third, we want to compare the psychological state of members of shamanistic religions with that of members of imported new religions.

Shamanistic religions are ecstatic (i.e., trance-based) religions. A central feature of such religions is the drama of a person being seized by the divine—a transcendental experience that is typically referred to as a trance or state of possession. Adherents of shamanistic religions believe that while mystics or shamans

---

[1]See Sudhir Kakar, *The Inner World: A Psycho-analytic Study of Childhood and Society in India*, 2d ed. (New York: Oxford University Press, 1981), p. 76.

are in the trance state they have direct experiential knowledge of the divine and can serve as channels of communication between the human community and the supernatural. In Japan shamans are understood to perceive "God's will" both through glossolalia ("speaking in tongues") and through receiving certain revelations or inspirations—including such things as prophesying, clairvoyance, and the transmission of messages from the dead.

The primal experiences reported by shamans include such things as visual and auditory hallucinations, waking visions and/or revelatory dreams, and spirit possession. These ecstatic experiences, especially spirit possession, may be either spontaneous or self-induced. Japanese shamans use *shugyo*, a practice involving strenuous bodily exercise, to induce trance states—states much like those that American Zen Buddhists achieve through meditation and Hare Krishnas achieve through chanting and dancing. Simple repetitive tasks, physical exhaustion, drugs, and other methods can all be used to bring on trance-like states.

So, primal experiences in shamanistic religions are much the same as primal experiences in our new religions. Trance states and experiences of spirit possession are in the modern Western context popularly referred to as altered states of consciousness and para-normal experiences, including such things as prophetic dreams, out-of-body experiences, encounters with the dead, seemingly miraculous healings, and supernatural knowledge. In both cultural contexts such experiences serve a similar purpose: they cause many people to join religious communities, because these groups offer explanations of what are otherwise inexplicable experiences; and they cause many such people to stay in their adopted religion because the community encourages them to continue having these experiences. Whatever we may think of the nature of these experiences, it is clear that many of the people who have them are convinced that they constitute evidence of the existence of a spiritual realm.

One of the most important issues for us as we consider these phenomena is the question of the mental health of those who report having had primal experiences. Many members of new religions resent the fact that the psychiatric profession has classified them mentally disturbed. Nevertheless, in many parts of the world it seems clear that individuals who become shamans have histories of having suffered primarily from what many in the West would describe as neurotic disorders, hysteria, and in some instances psychoses and schizophrenia. In other parts of the world such individuals have histories of having suffered primarily from consistent failure and social maladjustment. In many of these cases, the individuals report that their problems came under control when they became shamans. If this is the case, then there may be something about shamanic practices that could enlighten the mental health profession. In any case, it would seem that the relationship between the mental health profession and new religions could be mutually salutary if both sides would suspend judgment and refrain from actions based on premature conclusions.

PRIMAL EXPERIENCES AND MENTAL HEALTH

Primal experiences are universally reported by shamans and diviners. Looking closely at some examples of shamanism in the non-Western world should help us understand not only these spiritual experiences themselves but also their status in terms of the standards of traditional psychology. As a first example, we will consider the account of Okinawa shamans given by William P. Lebra in his paper "Shaman and Client in Okinawa."[2]

According to Okinawan beliefs, shamans (most of whom are women) are different from normal people from birth. They are born with a *kami*-spirit and are possessed by it, although they may not recognize that this is the case for some time. Individuals typically come to recognize that they are shamans following various notifications from *kami*-spirits. Initially these notifications take the form of strange occurrences, such as visual and auditory hallucinations and similar experiences. If the individual ignores these experiences, the *kami* sends a type of sickness that can't be diagnosed or cured by any modern or traditional doctors. After all else is tried, the only cure that remains is the seeking and acceptance of one's special *kami* or guardian spirit. Individuals who are thus cured are considered shamans; individuals who are not cured at this point are considered insane. Shamans subsequently learn which specific *kami* spirit possesses them through a dreamlike experience or hallucination.

We would stress the point that before individuals are recognized to be shamans, they are often considered to be mentally disturbed. Their parents and kin often express this worry quite openly even to researchers. But after they come to be recognized as shamans, their condition is reinterpreted. They are no longer

---

[2]Lebra, "Shaman and Client in Okinawa," in *Mental Health Research in Asia and the Pacific*, ed. William Caudill and Tsung-Yi Lin (Honolulu: East-West Center Press, 1969), pp. 216-22.

considered mentally disturbed but are held to be endowed with the capacity for spirit possession and the ability to see the past and the future. As mentioned in previous chapters, such a change in perception is reminiscent of that made by Anton T. Boisen concerning the patients in an American mental hospital.[3]

When would-be shamans recognize their potential to become shamans and yet refuse to accept the role, they are often regarded as continuing to suffer from behavioral disorders inflicted by their *kami*. Note that failure to accept the office of shaman is regarded as a symptom of a pathological condition, an indication that an individual is or is becoming insane. Once such people assume the office, their past behavior is reinterpreted as having been deviant in a divinely inspired fashion. Individuals who assume the office of shaman and then fail to carry out the duties of the office or behave too extravagantly are once more considered to be insane.

It is part of Okinawan belief that hopeless mental pathologies begin at birth and are punishment inflicted by the supernatural. People suffering from such pathologies may try to find a cure, but when they are unsuccessful, their affliction is ascribed to some irreparable wrong committed by ancestors. Less serious mental pathologies and simple behavioral disorders that arise later in life are held to be symptomatic of impaired relations with the supernatural. It is assumed that once the situation is accurately recognized and put right, the people will be cured.

Okinawan shamans cure their maladjustment by realizing their special status through a process of self-discovery and self-enlightenment with supernatural assistance. Two points should be emphasized. First, it is assumed that the supernatural may offer a cure when all else fails. And second, however their behavior or condition may have been perceived and described before, once individuals assume the role of shaman, their problem comes to be regarded as *religious* rather than psychological; the converted and enlightened will always be inclined to explain the problems experienced by shamans early in life in terms of their having been chosen.

Interestingly, we find the same sorts of maladjustment early in the lives of the leaders of many of the West's new religions that we find in the lives of the shamans. The "threat of failure" and

[3]Boisen, *The Exploration of the Inner World: A Study of Mental Disorder and Religious Experience* (1936; Philadelphia: University of Pennsylvania Press, 1971).

other complaints are a recurrent theme in the biographies of such individuals as the Mormon prophet Joseph Smith, John Humphrey Noyes of the Oneida Community, and the messianic figure of the Shaker community, Ann Lee. And similar descriptions apply, with small variations in the details, to the Reverend Sun Myung Moon, the Bhagwan Shree Rajneesh, Jim Jones of the ill-fated People's Temple cult in Jonestown, Guyana, and other leaders of recent new religions.

What we wish to emphasize here is the relative frequency of "failure" and maladjustment in the lives of those who later become shamans or cult figures—and the kind of knowledge that is required to overcome it.

We agree with the assertion John Calvin makes at the beginning of his *Institutes* that the form of knowledge that is most essential to living a full life—a form of knowledge that is unfortunately often discovered only after much failure and maladjustment—is *self-knowledge*. Regrettably, self-knowledge (and the means by which it is obtained—namely, *self-discovery*) is the form of knowledge that is most ignored in our system of formal education. On the whole, people in our culture's educational system acquire self-knowledge at most by means of nonverbal, unacknowledged, and unrewarded processes that are almost wholly incidental to the processes by which they acquire the formal thinking tools and skills to function in the larger world.

It is a rare individual who even becomes aware of this secondary learning process. It is a rarer individual still who is able to master both this secondary learning process and the formal educational system (especially in the sciences) and then goes on to become an educator who acknowledges, formalizes, and teaches self-knowledge or self-discovery. Our culture produces many more people who cannot meet this challenge, who are haunted by failure and maladjustment, by schismogeneses, and who are left searching for ways to achieve self-enlightenment. In our society, some of these people find it in the arts, in psychology, or through religion. But each of these options is still based primarily on reason and rationality, or is at least influenced by methods of science, and for some seekers that is itself the essential problem. Many of these individuals will be drawn to the occult in their search for solutions.

With this in mind, we should turn once more to Lebra's study of shamanism in Okinawa. He notes that the life histories of shamans reveal long records of discord in interpersonal relations. Their early life is characterized by frail health and recollections of playing alone, doing unusual things, and being slighted by parents. Their relations with kin tend to be strained and distant. Their marital life is marked by sexual incompatibility, frequent divorces, and bickering. Their ability to perform work and meet responsibilities is consistently poor. In short, the best single word to describe their early lives is *failure:* they meet with failure in home, school, occupation, sex, marriage, and life in general. Most important, however, is their failure in interpersonal relationships and general achievement. Poewe has noted much the same phenomena in the Herero of Namibia, among those who become "prophets"—individuals that might be described as Christianized shamans.[4] The major spirit that possesses them is Jesus. The Bible, fortuitously opened and inspiringly interpreted, leads them to their revelations.

Okinawa shamans, like Herero prophets, describe long bouts of illness that set them off from others. They recall these periods of illness as times of extreme anxiety, misery, and helplessness. In Namibia, most black women, but especially Herero women, suffer from unrelieved anxiety and helplessness. Those who do not themselves become "prophets" seek them out to be healed.

Another point that underscores the essential uniformity of the shamanistic experience around the world is the fact that the somatic disorders reported by the shamans in Okinawa are exactly the same as those that the Herero reported to Poewe. They commonly include generalized stomach disorders, prolonged and intense headaches, pounding noises, difficulties in breathing, pains or stiffness in the limbs (especially the legs), skin disorders, and sometimes hallucinatory experiences (seeing things, hearing voices, feeling as though their limbs or chests were in flames). They also described spells of dizziness or complete disorientation. Among the Herero, these symptoms occur frequently not only among those who become prophets but also among their clients. In addition, the Herero suffer from an unusually high and abnormally frequent occurrence of hypertension.

Both Herero prophets and Okinawa shamans report that all these conditions clear following conversion experiences. Likewise, Herero and Okinawa clients report improvement of their conditions after treatment. So it would seem religious conversion does offer psychotherapeutic improvement, whether real or

---

[4]Poewe, *The Namibian Herero: A History of Their Psychosocial Disintegration and Survival* (Lewiston, N.Y.: Edwin Mellen Press, 1985).

merely perceived. Stiffness, pain, partial paralyses, pounding headaches, roaring noises, skin afflictions, breathing problems, and other maladies disappear. Most importantly, when shamans and prophets accept their religious office, adopting a new understanding of their whole lifetime experience, including failures, inadequacies, illnesses, and misfortunes, as being supernaturally imposed, it all begins to make sense to them for the first time.

SHAMANS, SPIRIT POSSESSION, AND THE ISSUE OF PSYCHIATRIC EPISODES

Sasaki has described the shaman as a

> medium between the human and the supernatural world
> . . . who communicates freely as a human medium with the
> "heavenly world" where goods and good spirits reside, and
> with the "underworld" where the devils reside . . . ,
> through offering sacrifices or doing prayers to the super-
> natural spirits and bringing himself to the state of trance
> and thus makes prophecy or even cures the illness of the
> clients.[5]

Usually, shamanism involves a trance state induced at will. When a shamanic tradition exists in a society, shamanism may be a vocation like any other. In most situations becoming a shaman requires rigorous training. In Japan, as we have noted, this training is called *shugyo*, "self-training." It entails learning by means of repetition a number of simple body movements and sensory stimulations that will induce a trance. Repetitious movements and sensory stimulations bring about a gradual dimming of both physiological and psychological consciousness, leading to a diminution of ego activities. Trance can also be brought on through extreme exhaustion caused by hypoglycemia.

In South America, becoming a shaman also requires training. Children grow up in a shamanic tradition and consider shamanism a plausible career choice. In this part of the world, training involves seclusion, reduced diets, and ingestion of hallucinogens. Because group therapy is emphasized, shamans must be talented at dramatically indicating the presence of the spirits that possess them. Audrey Butt has noted that good-looking young men with a ready understanding, a good sense of humor,

---

[5]Sasaki, "Psychiatric Study of the Shaman in Japan," in *Mental Health Research in Asia and the Pacific*, ed. William Caudill and Tsung-Yi Lin (Honolulu: East-West Center Press, 1969), pp. 223-41.

and a personality that sets them above their peers are most likely to succeed as shamans. "Successful shamans are lively, intelligent and responsive to others, quick to see the implications of every social situation."[6] Clearly the shamans in this tradition have very different personalities than those in the Japanese shamanic tradition or the South African and Namibian prophetic tradition.

Shamanic styles are significantly shaped by the tradition, specific social and cultural setting, and individual and social health problems of the setting in which they develop. In South America shamans are more frequently male than female; in China and Japan it is the reverse. I. M. Lewis attributes some of these differences in shamanic style to the fact that in some social settings only women and men of subordinate social status become shamans. He also makes a significant distinction between *peripheral amoral possession cults* and *central morality cults.*[7]

Peripheral cults are usually protest cults that allow the underprivileged to heal themselves and/or make demands on their masters. The shamans of these cults are different from shamans in societies where *moralistic tribal religions* are fully functional, as in the South American setting we have been describing. Shamans in *moralistic tribal religions,* which are found in South America and North and East Africa, are principally concerned with the moral order of their people, with the relationships between one person and another and with the relationship of all people to the earth. During ritual séances, these possessed shamans exhort people to shun evils of incest, adultery, sorcery, and homicide and to be harmonious in their social relations. Such shamans are carefully selected and trained, although they too follow the typical path to accepting their office: they dream strange dreams that persuade them of the correctness of their choice and seek seclusion in the forest to better communicate with the spiritual world.

Public morality cults are one type of the new religions we have described in previous chapters. They tend to develop in societies with great standing religious traditions such as Christianity or Islam, especially in periods of rapid social change. Individuals or a class of socially mobile people whose ambitions are at odds with the prevailing way of life form these new religious move-

---

[6]Butt, "Training to Be a Shaman," in *Trances,* by A. Butt, S. Wavell, and N. Epton (London: Allen & Unwin, 1966).
[7]Lewis, *Ecstatic Religion: An Anthropological Study of Spirit Possession and Shamanism* (Harmondsworth: Penguin, 1971), pp. 129-48.

ments, the leaders of which resemble those who become shamans in tribal settings. Like shamans, these leaders become possessed, although their possession often begins as an illness and ends not merely with a cure but with what they interpret as divine inspiration. Leaders with a gifted imagination or an extraordinary capacity for fantasy will elaborate their divine inspiration, as Joseph Smith did in the *Book of Mormon* and the Reverend Moon did in the *Divine Principle*. Fawn M. Brodie has described Smith's reaction to his inspiration as follows:

> His imagination spilled over like a spring freshet. When he stared into his crystal and saw gold in every odd-shaped hill, he was escaping from the drudgery of farm labor into a glorious opulence. Had he been able to continue his schooling, subjecting his plastic fancy and tremendous dramatic talent to discipline and molding, his life might never have taken the exotic turn it did. His mind was agile and eager, and disciplined study might have caused his creative talents to turn in a more conventionally profitable direction.[8]

At this point we should take note of the fact that there are significant themes in the case histories of shamans and members of new religions generally. These themes are *not* aspects of what the traditional Western psychological community would characterize as psychopathological in nature but would describe instead as evidence of the discontent that is often found in very bright though undisciplined people. Included are such motifs as a desire to escape from the drudgery or the tortures of everyday life, a hankering for enhanced status or being considered special, a fertile but undisciplined imaginative or fantasy life, dramatic talent, and little or incomplete education and molding. We have already noted that many of the young adults who join new religions have had some college education but that few have fully completed it.

Now let us look more closely at Sasaki's careful study of shamans in different districts of Japan.[9] He determined that the main function of these shamans is to prophesy, conveying the "divine will" from a "god" to a client. Ideally, shamans are in a state of trance when they prophesy. They also stage magical rituals, at which time they tell folktales in amusing and dramatic ways. Finally, shamans function as mediums to communicate with the

---

[8]Brodie, *No Man Knows My History* (New York: Knopf, 1963).
[9]Sasaki, "Psychiatric Study of the Shaman in Japan."

dead when called upon to do so by their clients.

Of the fifty-six shamans Sasaki interviewed, forty were women. Most of them were past the age of forty. Most were poorly educated. Thirty-seven percent had somewhat more than six years of schooling, but forty-seven percent had less than six years of schooling, and nineteen percent had no formal schooling at all. In terms of income, these shamans fell into the middle or working class. A few (four percent) were upper-class; fewer yet (three percent) were really lower-class.

Most of these shamans experienced full spirit possession only once, after which their trance and possession experiences generally diminished. During their initial experience, most displayed a transformation of personality involving glossolalia that was often accompanied by vivid sensory experiences of a revelatory nature. In later life, glossolalia deteriorated into an act and revelation became nothing more than attaching meanings to ideas or symbols that arose randomly in the shaman's mind. Lebra notes that some of the shamans he studied felt pressured by their clients to go into a trance when they couldn't or didn't want to do so. When they capitulated by putting on a trance-like act, some of these shamans felt uncomfortable, fearing their insincerity.

As we have noted, the "prophets" in the independent churches of South Africa, which are syncretistic but heavily influenced by Christianity, are essentially Christianized shamans. They constitute an evolution toward greater freedom in shamanistic practice. These prophets typically have one revelatory vision that imbues them with a sense of mission "to help their people," but after that they do not feel any pressure to go into a trance. They draw on "the power of Christ" and randomly select passages from the Bible to help them to arrive at penetrating insights about the condition of their client.

Among Japanese and Chinese shamans, Sasaki and P. M. Yap have recognized three degrees of possession, which they characterize as follows: (1) *complete* possession, which is characterized by "clouding of consciousness, skin anaesthesia to pain, a changed demeanor and tone of voice, the impossibility of recalling the patient to reality, and subsequent amnesia"; (2) *partial* possession, which is characterized by "mild clouding, partial anaesthesia, no change in voice and demeanor, the possibility of recall to reality, and partial amnesia subsequently"; and (3) *histrionic* possession, which is characterized by an absence of all the evidences of true possessions. Among possessed female patients, they noted that "giggling, belching and other attention-seeking devices" often accompanied episodes of histrionic possession. Some patients also engaged in such activities as involuntary twisting of the neck, chanting, shutting of the eyes, lying stuporously on the ground, rolling about, climbing up windows, panting, somersaulting, walking on knees, and so on. Some acted in imitation of the "personality" of the possessing "spirit."[10] In Japan, apparently in contrast to other areas, a trance state precedes states of ecstasy.

After assembling intensive life history interviews, Sasaki was able to define two principal ways of achieving possession. One is through *shugyo*, or self-training; the other is a matter of *spontaneous* possession. Importantly, Sasaki distinguishes between two categories of spontaneous possession. The first category is the rarer of the two, occurring in only five of the fifty-six individuals he interviewed, in individuals whose initial possessed state was free of any other psychopathological syndrome. These shamans had been subjected to severe suffering in their preshamanic days and at a critical point became possessed, which effected a cure of their ills. One woman, for instance, had been married to a dominant but unemployed man. Following a trance, she suddenly assumed the dominant role in the marriage and thereafter in matters of religious beliefs.

Sasaki detected the second category of spontaneous possession in eleven of the fifty-six interviewees, in individuals who had experienced periodic transient psychoses in both their preshamanic and shamanic careers. Spirit possession in these people seemed to be associated with what Yap has called "reactive psychosis." The subjects reported having suffered from numbness of extremities, agitation, and in general the sorts of symptoms we have already described as occurring among the Herero of Namibia and the shamans of Okinawa. These individuals came from extremely difficult backgrounds, were poorly educated or uneducated, and entered states of clouded consciousness (trance) when they encountered particularly serious problems. Many of them found that possession or trance was very helpful in solving these problems. Among the Herero, malignant or acute anxiety and panic were common among those women who sought the help of "prophets."

At this point we might note some similarities between Lewis's and Sasaki's formulations of the categories of shamans

---

[10]See Sasaki and Yap, in *Mental Health Research in Asia and the Pacific*.

and possession or trance. Lewis's description of *peripheral* possession resembles Sasaki's description of *spontaneous* possession. Both can be subdivided as Sasaki suggests. What Lewis calls main morality religions, be they main morality possession cults or new religions, resemble Sasaki's *shugyo* shamanistic religions. Both involve disappointed individuals who are alienated or tortured by real life and who seek to escape through *shugyo* or other techniques, such as the sorts of meditation and chanting that are practiced in the new religions. No pathologies at all need be associated with this type of shaman or seeker. They experience life as a problem. Leaders often hear voices that outline for them a mission. Some successful Herero "prophets" resemble *shugyo*-type shamans, but their "apostles" and clients do not. Table 2 (p. 143) lists the types of possession and shamans along with some of their characteristics.

Of the fifty-six shamans Sasaki studied, forty fell into the self-trained category, five into the spontaneous-reversal category, and eleven into the spontaneous-reactive category. The most successful and revered shamans were those in the spontaneous-reactive category.

Of the forty shamans in the *shugyo* category, Sasaki mentions that thirty had no psychopathic symptoms, four were hebephrenic schizophrenics, another four had personality disorders, one suffered from alcoholic psychosis, and one suffered from general paresis. Of the five shamans in the spontaneous-reversal category, four had personality disorders and one was a paranoid schizophrenic. Of the eleven shamans in the spontaneous-reactive category, eight had reactive psychoses (i.e., transient psychotic episodes at critical times in their lives that helped them solve their problems), two had personality disorders, and one suffered from catatonic schizophrenia.

If we include periodic and temporary reactive psychoses, then forty-six percent of these shamans had psychological problems that they apparently mastered while they were shamans. Fifty-four percent overcame difficult life situations without developing psychological problems.

We have now noted at some length that symptoms of anxiety, social maladjustment, and somatic complaints are common among shamans, "prophets," and their clients. Collectively, these symptoms were in the past referred to by the general term *hysteria*. We will be discussing this collection of neurotic disorders in greater detail later. At this point we would simply note that contemporary psychologists discuss hysteria in terms of more clearly

Table 2
Types of Possession and Shamans

	SELF-TRAINED TYPE	SPONTANEOUS (OR PERIPHERAL) TYPES	
		Spontaneous-reversal	Spontaneous-reactive
Social aspects	Critical of main society, seeks to escape harsh reality, achieve higher social status, start own cult or movement or join alternative cult	Deprivation, oppression, severe suffering	Severe deprivation, feels overwhelmed
Psychological aspects	Usually no pathology, but signs of discontent, disappointment, alienation, low self-esteem, anomalous experiences.	Usually prone to no pathology, but prone to conflicts over every-day problems, mild temporary neurotic anxiety, personality disorders	Some psychopathological symp-toms, usually reactive psychosis, malignant anxiety, severe guilt, sometimes mental confusion, restlessness
Physical health aspects	No pathology	No pathology; hypochondria	Headaches, general aches and pains, temporary paralyses, general stomach complaints, breathing problems
	Sociocultural factors play key role	Preshamanic personality factors play key role	

defined subcategories, including alienation or dissociative disorders, histrionic and other personality disorders, psychoses (especially reactive psychosis), and other functional disorders.

In the West, the definition of hysteria and the understanding of its manifestations have changed through the centuries. In addition, it has been noted that different manifestations of hysteria occur in every culture and that they become a mass phenomenon during periods of cultural and social chaos resulting from such things as war, intercultural contact, and epidemics. Hysteria also manifests itself differently in different social classes. Members of the Western working class—or rather of its dispossessed—still typically exhibit somatic manifestations. By contrast, the middle and upper-middle classes complain about mental or psychological problems and identity crises. Many develop behavioral or personality disorders, but few mention physical aches and pains as part of their hysterical complaints. The reason for the great variety of manifestations of hysteria has to do with suggestion. Great suggestibility and a deep sense of moral injustice are the essence of hysteria, and hysterics are sensitive, even if unconsciously so, to what sorts of symptoms are acceptable or fashionable and likely to arouse sympathy.

The phenomena we have called primal experiences are basically culturally embellished symptoms of hysteria. If shamans, "prophets," and leaders of new religions do not manifest one or another form of "hysteria" themselves, then they are at least very sensitive to its prevalence in a good proportion of the population. Leaders' abilities to "dramatize" and their followers' susceptibility to such dramatization create a powerful bond between them. At the bottom of many hysterical problems is an *idee fixe* that will tend to make most "hysterics" very devoted and even fanatical followers.

Cured hysterics or shamans who have mastered their spirits often become spokespeople for their time. A classic example of this is Bertha Pappenheim, a Viennese woman who was cured of her hysteria in 1882 and went on to become an accomplished writer and champion of the Jewish feminist cause. So revered was she that in 1954, eighteen years after her death, the West German government issued a stamp honoring her memory.

The case of Bertha Pappenheim suggests two important points. First, her predicament arose from the suffocating situation in which this exceptionally intelligent and lively woman grew up. She felt a deep sense of injustice at being forced to terminate her education when she was sixteen and spend a good part of her youth caring for an invalid father while her less intelligent brother attended law school. Second, if we can show sympathy for Pappenheim, then we should also show sympathy for present-day hysterics who manifest vaguer forms of character disorders and depression that arise from the protean historical circumstances of our own time.

SOCIOCULTURAL AND PSYCHOLOGICAL FACTORS AMONG THOSE WHO JOIN TODAY'S NEW RELIGIONS

In some societies shamanism is a system. As S. M. Shirokogoroff has shown, shamanism is based on specific assumptions about spirits and the spirit world.[11] From these, shamans derive hypotheses about which spirits might have caused a condition. In trances, they act out their hypotheses, and the subsequent improvement of their clients confirms their hypotheses (or proves them incorrect).

Some shamans are trained in meditation techniques. Others depend more on hallucinogens. In some areas of the world trance or ecstasy is primary; in others, possession is primary. In some societies shamans experience trance and possession only once; in other societies shamans reach possessions repeatedly, driven on by vigorous dancing, music, and audience participation. Some shamans become practitioners following mental and/or physical health problems; others choose it to escape an unpleasant or impoverished life.

During the 1970s and '80s, aspects of shamanism have been introduced into the eclectic mix of practices, beliefs, and dogmas that constitute emerging new religions. Some new religions recognize the spirit world that in shamanistic religions is understood to be mastered by shamans. Other new religions simply practice the ecstatic expressions of shamanism—shaking, dancing, rolling, aggression, group drama, and so on.

As we have already noted, different individuals report having had different kinds of primal experiences prior to having joined their new religions. Members of the Unification Church seem to have more primal experiences (or at least to recognize them more openly) after they join. Of seventy-four members of the Unification Church in the New York City area responding to a

[11]Shirokogoroff, *Psychomental Complex of the Tungus* (New York: AMS Press, 1980).

questionnaire in 1979 and an additional eight who were orally interviewed between October 1978 and June 1980, sixty (73 percent) said that they had had primal experiences, including visions, revelatory dreams, and hearing voices. Twenty-two (27 percent) said they had had no such mystical experiences. Of those who had primal experiences, thirty-two percent described having had visions of Sun Myung Moon in various personally meaningful postures. Others reported having had visions of Jesus or feeling and seeing the presence of God in everything. Some saw faces of people of various cultures or of a beautiful house being built. They interpreted these visions as having to do with Unification goals of interethnic marriages, brotherhood, and world restoration. Some had visions and encounters with dead relatives. Others had experiences that foretold events. Still others reported heightened self-awareness, visions of spirits, physical contact with spirits, spiritual smells, sensual awareness, revelation, and so on.

Hare Krishna members typically have histories of having been heavily into drug mysticism before joining. After they have joined the movement, their primal experiences come from the sound of the mantra, which helps them achieve Krishna consciousness.

Few Rajneeshies report primal experiences of the sort that members of the Unification Church report, except for reports by some that they have heard a voice that seems to come "from someone else and somewhere else." Some report having had "peak experiences"—experiences of extreme elation, of oneness, "of everything being part of everything else"—before they joined. But most report some sort of ecstatic experience, especially those who met the Bhagwan Shree Rajneesh during the early days in Poona. These individuals say that what happened to them is indescribable. One reported, "I went out of my head and into my heart." According to Bob Mullan, many felt a deep sense of having "come home." One woman reported having put a *mala* over her head and said it "felt like an electric current going through me." Some described tranquility and "weeks and weeks of bliss," an experience completely divorced from logic.[12]

Some of the experiences reported by Rajneeshies sound very much like the expressions of hysteria that occur among would-be shamans. Mullan relates many such cases, including

---

[12]Mullan, *Life as Laughter* (London: Routledge & Kegan Paul, 1983), pp. 66, 71, 75, 79.

that of one man who described having gone for a period being unable to speak and later having "got paranoid." Paranoia is a common complaint among these individuals. Some report anxiety attacks, or having "felt insane," or describe a life of "fear." Others report lengthy periods of "depression" and "nervous breakdowns" (sometimes their own, sometimes those of a parent). Both men and women describe "weeks of crying" or "crying all the time." Personality disorders are especially prominent. One man describes his having gone to a school for "disturbed children" and acknowledges that he attempted suicide, stole, shoplifted, was arrested for possession of drugs and put on probation, and so on. Another man describes himself as having been a problem case. He was expelled from school, had shallow relationships, and says he often "felt hopeless." A woman describes shallow love relationships, wife swapping, divorce, having been beaten by her father and later by her husband, and so on. Some women had unsettled marriages, left husbands, had "wild times with lots of men," "fell apart," felt insane, took therapy, and so on. Most were heavily into therapy of all kinds and the occult before they joined the Rajneeshies.

It is clear that members of new religions describe their primal experiences in the language of their specific movements, and it is also clear that they follow a format acceptable to the group. But apart from the cosmetic differences that these factors would naturally introduce into their reports of their primal experiences, there are also significant differences in the *substance* of primal experiences from one new religion to another. Under the humor and laughter of the Rajneeshies lie real psychological disturbances that are not similarly present among members of the Unification Church, for example.

Moreover, the differences between the primal experiences of Rajneeshies and members of the Unification Church correlate with differences in age, relationship experiences, life experiences, and so on. In Mullan's words, "the 'average' Rajneeshie is 'middle-class,' well-educated, professionally qualified, has been divorced at least once, has suffered a 'personal crisis,' has been through mysticism, drugs, politics, feminism, and is 'thirtyish'— in short, the counter-culturist brought up to date."[13]

In addition, Mullan's interviews show that before the Rajneeshies joined their new religion, many of them shifted in and out of schools, homes, jobs, and professions—in short experi-

---

[13]Mullan, *Life as Laughter*, pp. 50-51.

encing a general restlessness. By contrast, members of the Unification Church tend to be somewhat younger and have lived less
colorful lives. Most seem to have come from more stable homes
and had fewer sexual, drug, and therapy experiences. Rajneeshies
tend to want to experience the here and now fully. Unificationists
tend to be end-seekers, solution-oriented, and future-oriented.
They generally cling to fixed points of identity such as a moral
code, family, social action, and the ideal of perfectionism.
Unificationists tend to take global issues seriously in ways that
Rajneeshies do not. All of these distinctions apply to the two religions in their present state only. Early members of the American
Unification Church—those who joined in the 1960s—reported
histories not unlike those of Rajneeshies.[14]

The primal experiences of Unification Church members
that we described earlier were taken from interviews conducted
by McGowan in New York City. Now we would like to take a look
at some of the primal experiences that members of the Unification Church in California described to John Lofland.

Miss Lee (a pseudonym) was Moon's emissary in America.
She reported having suffered from bouts of depression during her
early teens. She recalled sitting on a secluded hilltop and "receiving visions, hearing voices, and generally hallucinating," and she
said that she continued to have such experiences. She noted that
she had rejected much of an early Methodist training and that she
had been deeply influenced by the spiritualistic writings of
Emanuel Swedenborg, who she said appeared "to her in visions."
Imbued with a sense of mission that was confirmed by her spirit,
but resisting the religious path, Lee "fell ill with chronic diarrhea
(a common hysterical symptom) and eventually nephritis, both of
which resisted all medical treatment. After two years of this, her
health was broken and she was completely bedridden."[15] Her
condition improved after she saw Sun Myung Moon and took up
his cause. On the whole, Lee's story is a classic case study of a shaman or a hysteric.

The primal experiences of Americans tend not to be quite so
fascinating. One early joiner reported "frequent ecstatic religious
experiences." Her case also has some resemblance to hysteria,
for she described homosexual panic and periods of seclusion
spent in "crying and moaning." She reported that following her

[14]On this, see John Lofland, *Doomsday Cult* (New York: Irvington, 1984),
pp. 31-49.
[15]Lofland, *Doomsday Cult*, p. 35.

homosexual episode she had "private religious hallucinations, including sanctification—being made holy and free of all sin."[16]

Some scholars insist that hysteria no longer occurs in the modern West. Symptoms of hysteria are usually culturally specific and often learned by daughters from mothers. In light of the changes in that relationship in our culture, it may simply be that we are now evidencing private, subdued, fragmented aspects of the condition. On the other hand, these milder symptoms may be evidences of what P. M. Yap has described as culture-bound reactive psychosis.[17]

Lofland also presents the case of an N.R.O.T.C. cadet who claimed to have undergone "a series of religious and hallucinatory experiences" while at sea, one of which involved "fiery red balls." It is interesting that this young man "was highly ambivalent about his homosexuality, unable to explain it, unable to accept it, and unable to quit it."[18]

Another man, who reported having been a frontline combat soldier in Nazi Germany, was haunted by "super-real" dreams. The dreams seemed to be replays of his wartime experiences, but he felt that both the dreams and an accompanying sensation "that someone—or thing" was constantly behind him but "would be gone when he turned around" needed further explanation. He "started reading about spiritualism and attending spiritualist churches." What he could not find in the occult he found in the Unification Church—namely, "an encompassing meaning and direction to his life."[19]

The life of another young man who joined the Unification Church was filled more with delusions than hallucinations. He was virtually illiterate and he flunked out after his first year at a university, but he nevertheless clung to the belief that he was an intellectual and would be a learned man and inventor. He collected a library including occult periodicals. He could not sustain a conversation, frequently seemed to forget what he was talking about, had severe interaction problems, looked constantly at his feet, and increasingly withdrew from contact.

Another young man spoke of having become fat, prone to bruises, and hyperactive when he was in the tenth grade. Although his condition was corrected medically, he remained a

[16]Lofland, *Doomsday Cult*, pp. 34-36.
[17]Yap, "The Possession Syndrome: A Comparison of Hong Kong and French Findings," *Journal of Mental Science* 106 (1960): 114-37.
[18]Lofland, *Doomsday Cult*, pp. 36-37.
[19]Lofland, *Doomsday Cult*, p. 37.

150   **Understanding Cults and New Religions**

loner, fascinated with the apocalyptic books of the Bible, extreme right-wing political literature, and strict moral codes.

A young woman born to hillbilly farmers and married at age fifteen began speaking in tongues and falling into trances that would last for hours while attending tent meetings. These activities stopped when she became preoccupied with the raising of three children. Confused about her sexuality, she appears to have hoped that joining the Unification Church would improve her marital situation.

Finally, Lofland mentions the case of a young man who dropped in and out of junior college, felt estranged and alone, and became a recluse. He supported himself by working in a plywood plant but had the dream of building a financial empire. His life showed typical shamanistic patterns of failure and reliance on the occult.

We find evidence of similar tensions and aspirations with shamans as with members of the Unification Church. So acute are these tensions that they become central in the lives of the individuals who experience them. We might also note that these people are similar in their refusal to accept defeat or accept professional judgments concerning their conditions. They all cling to a sense of their own worth even when they find it supported only by the occult or, later, a new religion. It should be clear that many symptoms reported in Lofland's studies of members of the Unification Church (and, by extension, members of other new religions) are simply modern manifestations of what earlier generations referred to as hysteria.

WITCHCRAFT, SORCERY, AND SHAMANISM: SOCIOLOGICAL AND PSYCHOLOGICAL ASPECTS

Concerned primarily with the sociological aspects of these phenomena, I. M. Lewis has made some significant distinctions between witchcraft and spirit possession.[20] He argues that when spirit possession of the peripheral or spontaneous type occurs among members of subordinate social classes, it typically affects both men and women, and the possessed individuals often use it to make demands on superiors. When possession occurs among the more privileged classes, women are possessed more often.

Even when witchcraft practices occur in societies that also believe in shamanism, they are typically found in different social

---

[20]See Lewis, *Ecstatic Religion*.

contexts. Accusations of witchcraft are usually made by individuals against their equals or by superiors against inferiors. In polygynous societies, a man's wives sometimes accuse one another of bewitchment, or the husband may accuse his wives of practicing witchcraft against him. On the other hand, when wives collectively conspire against their common husband, they typically use spirit possession. During the Middle Ages in Europe, it was usually men who accused women, either betrayed lovers or wives, of having bewitched them.

It is important to note that witchcraft and shamanism occur only in special social and cultural contexts. Generally speaking, such beliefs thrive in social contexts that are hierarchical in nature, whether the hierarchy is based on age or status or some other form of seniority. The cultural contexts that support such beliefs are typically marked by a prevalence of mythologies that emphasize spirits, demons, ghosts, and the like. As Ilza Veith has noted, the most important factor in the decline of traditional "medicine was the growing influence of mysticism, not only upon the population at large but also upon the educated."[21] During periods of successive waves of epidemics, famine, or other natural disasters, such as those that occurred in the Roman Empire in the second and third centuries, medicine and medical practitioners have typically been overwhelmed and unable to cope. Not unexpectedly, people have become very susceptible to promises of faith healing in such circumstances. In addition, as monotheistic religions (especially Christianity) grew in influence, people began to blame diseases and disasters on demons.

The popular preoccupation with demonology and witchcraft persisted and rose to a fever pitch after the publication in 1494 of *Malleus Maleficarum*, also known as the *Witches Hammer*. This book ushered in an era of witch executions that did not subside in Europe until the 1600s and in New England until the 1700s. Reports suggest that most individuals accused of being witches in Europe were women suffering from hysteria.

The association between hysteria and witchcraft in the European context and between hysteria and spirit-possession in other parts of the world, such as China, Korea, Japan, New Guinea, and parts of Africa, requires some clarification. Some aspects of hysteria are relatively universal, while other aspects are culturally specific. In the past, too many symptoms were identified as aspects of hysteria. Today our culture seems to have overreacted

---

[21]Veith, *Hysteria* (Chicago: University of Chicago Press, 1965).

to this emphasis, attributing the symptoms to such a variety of other syndromes as to suggest that hysteria no longer exists in the West. We now talk about conversion disorders, dissociative disorders, borderline personality disorders, and so on. In the Third World, Yap favors the term "reactive psychosis."

In this context, we are satisfied with Alex Sinclair's definition of hysteria as a "neurotic mechanism which an individual unconsciously uses in order to avoid the psychological distress associated with emotional conflict,"[22] although we prefer the term *schismogenesis* to "emotional conflict." We have already noted the relationship of the four schismogeneses to new religions. Relational schismogenesis, for example, is similar to some of the borderline personality disorders that we observed in Mullan's life histories. Rational schismogenesis is similar to alienation or dissociative disorders. Spiritual schismogenesis is analogous to the notion of culture-bound reactive psychosis. And emotional schismogenesis describes well the current expression of hysteria in the Third World. Of course, as we have noted elsewhere, our enumeration of the four schismogeneses is simply a heuristic device. We are not suggesting that a given individual will not suffer from more than one of them at the same time.

Sinclair's definition of hysteria is simple and clear. He also notes that hysteria can be "accompanied by physical correlates such as paralysis, blindness, inability to speak, deafness, and so on." Because mind and body are rarely separated in Africa, for example, mental distress is usually expressed in somatic terms. Langness and Sinclair also argue "that because of the natives' heightened suggestibility, which is associated with their strong beliefs in magic and the supernatural, they are ideally suited for hysterical mechanisms."[23]

By analogy, we would argue that the susceptibility of members of new religions is similarly heightened and that they express their mental and emotional distress or conflict in the verbal and body language of their particular group. Whatever a member ponders and emphasizes in his or her life history, be it identity crisis, life crisis, relationship problems, or whatever, it is usually sorted out and described in terms of the dogma (if any exists) or ritual or language of the group. The common feature among to-

---

[22]Sinclair, quoted by L. L. Langness in "Hysterical Psychosis in the New Guinea Highlands: a Bena Bena Example," *Psychiatry* 28 (1965): 258-77.

[23]See Langness, "Hysterical Psychosis in the New Guinea Highlands," pp. 258-77.

ThePsychology of Shamanism 153

day's new religions is the fact that these individuals express in
personalized form a psychological unease that is clearly associated with post-1960 middle-class life. Just as in New Guinea hysteria is clearly associated with men of a certain age and category
who experienced situation-specific stress, and just as in Europe
hysteria was once associated primarily with women of the leisured classes, so today the symptoms of hysteria are associated
with middle-class women and men of a certain age and category
who experience stress specific to their class and private situation.

Thomas Sydenham, a practicing physician in England in the
1600s, argued that hysteria has nothing to do with insanity. He described "the incurable despair of patients, their belief that they
must suffer all the evil that befalls mankind, their presentiment of
further unhappiness." He discussed, as Veith points out, "their
propensity to anger, jealousy, and suspicion and pointed to their
very occasional intervals of joy, hope, and cheerfulness; their day-
time moods, mirrored by their dreams, were haunted by sad forebodings." "All is caprice," said Sydenham, "they love without
measure those whom they will soon hate without reason." Veith
goes on to point out that "with deep compassion for these patients, Sydenham compared their physical and mental sufferings
to life in a purgatory wherein they expiate crimes committed in a
previous state." And she notes his emphasis that "those who thus
suffer are persons of prudent judgment, persons who in their pro-
fundity of meditations and the wisdom of their speech far surpass
those whose minds have never been exerted by such stimuli."[24]

---

[24]Veith, *Hysteria*, pp. 137-47.

10

Magical Religions, Hysteria, and Christianity

NEW RELIGIONS OR MAGICAL RELIGIONS?

The general theory of religion propounded by Rodney Stark and William S. Bainbridge predicts that people who are denied access to desired rewards will tend to accept either specific or general "compensators" instead.[1] Specific compensators include such things as ritual procedures prescribed by a shaman to cure a specific condition, such as warts. General compensators include such things as the promise of a happy life. Compensators usually entail promises of rewards in the distant future or in some other nonverifiable context.

Religion, says Stark, "is a system of general compensators based on supernatural assumptions," and he contends that those religious organizations that move "markedly in the direction of non-supernaturalism" will thereby "pursue the path to ruin."[2] On the other hand, Bainbridge presents evidence that Transcendental Meditation (TM) decreased in popularity as it moved in the di-

---

[1]See Stark and Bainbridge, *The Future of Religion: Secularization, Revival and Cult Formation* (Berkeley and Los Angeles: University of California Press, 1985), pp. 7, 30, 172, 265, 285..

[2]Stark, "Must All Religions be Supernatural?" in *The Social Impact of New Religious Movements*, ed. Bryan Wilson (New York: Rose of Sharon Press, 1981), pp. 159-77.

rection of promising increased supernatural power.[3] He contends that the drop in recruitment began before the intensifica-
tion of the religious element, but the fact of the matter is that TM
originally gained large numbers of recruits precisely because it
emphasized its "scientific" status and sought to avoid the label of
religion. It was presented as an intellectually respectable if novel
technique of personal development. While the later drop in recruitment is attributable to a number of factors, it seems quite
clear that important among them is the fact that an increased
number of magical claims—promises to practitioners of everything from a knowledge of the past and the future to the ability to
levitate—belied its claim to being science-based. When its supposedly scientifically proven claim of offering a new state of consciousness was debunked, it lost those who had joined it for that
reason. University students who had found it respectable to practice magic so long as everyone considered it a science lost interest in it when its true status was revealed.

In general we disagree with Stark and Bainbridge's market
model of new religions, although we do agree that new religions,
new psychologies, and new therapies are all marketed in our culture. Indeed, we would go so far as to suggest that the secular-
religious dichotomy is not vital in the discussion of new religions.
In a sense, the term "new religion" is a misnomer, since so-called
new religions are not actually new products taking the place of
old ones in a religious market. The thing that is "new" in new religions is the content of their mythological idioms.

New religions are simply recent versions of experiential
therapo-religious phenomena. Throughout history there has
been a continuous waxing and waning of medico-moral, or
therapo-religious, or therapo-spiritual cults. They existed before
the time of Christ, and they still exist in all parts of the world. If we
want to make a distinction, we might better distinguish between
experiential therapo-religious phenomena on one hand and *intellectual* therapo-religious phenomena on the other. Experience
and magic predominate in the one, rationality and faith in the
other. The former tends to be magical, the latter discursive.
Throughout history, each has borrowed from the other. Medico-
moral religions have incorporated aspects of therapo-religious
cults, for example. It is because sociologists tend not to engage in

---

[3]Bainbridge and Jackson, "The Rise and Decline of Transcendental Meditation," in *The Social Impact of New Religious Movements*, pp. 135-58.

comparative or historical studies that they have assigned an exaggerated importance to contemporary new religions.

Throughout history, therapo-spiritual cults have had to steer a dangerous course—first between traditional medical practice and formal mainline religions, then between science and mainline religions, and finally between state and church. The legal battles in which today's new religions are embroiled—concerning issues of brainwashing, whether they are secular or religious, and so on—resemble those in which the Mesmer cult was caught up two centuries ago in France and Austria. Indeed, cults in all times and places have faced such opposition. Given the current separation between state and church and and between science and religion, we should not be surprised by the legal opposition they are facing. Generally speaking, experiential therapo-spiritual cults are considered untidy religious mutants in our culture, and the courts seem to offer a perfectly rational context in which to handle the embarrassingly irrational problems.

In order to clarify our contention that most contemporary new religions follow a long line of therapo-moral cults that have stressed experience more than doctrine, we should look at some historical examples of such cults—specifically, the Aesculapian cult of ancient Greece and the Mesmer cult of the eighteenth century.

The Aesculapian cult of the Hippocratic period of ancient Greece is a good example of the sorts of therapo-moral cults that have existed for centuries in the interstices between the medical professions and religious institutions. At its center was the practice of "temple healing" facilitated by its god of medicine, Aesculapius. Like members of the Unification Church who have visions of the Reverend Sun Myung Moon, members of the Aesculapian cult had dreams and visions of Aesculapius that encouraged their belief in his cures and beneficence. And just as the Unification Church encourages its members to write up and circulate their dreams, so members of the Aesculapian cult recorded on votive tablets at the temple sites the dreams and visions experienced by patients during their temple sleep.

Ilza Veith has argued that suggestion probably played a major part in the Aesculapian temple healing process. There is good evidence that some temple priests impersonated Aesculapius in encounters with semi-conscious patients. Veith also contends that priests may have enhanced the suggestibility of patients by staging dramatic rituals of sham surgery. Like today's faith healers, they may also have used hypnosis. Since many patients were hysterics, they were already receptive to mystical and ritualistic procedures of temple healing. The need for "moral treatment" or "moral therapy" of hysterics was noted by several physicians in Europe throughout the centuries.

The Mesmer cult, which gained substantial popularity in Vienna and Paris in the late eighteenth century, is another interesting example of a therapo-moral cult. Central to Mesmerism was the concept "magnetic fluid"—a feature that has obvious counterparts in contemporary cults and new religions, such as the "engramic clearing" of Scientology, the "somatic clearing" of Zulu diviners, and the "energy" and "merging" of Rajneeshies. Indeed, if the notion of "magnetic fluid" is replaced with that of "energy," the resemblance between Mesmerism and Rajneeshism is strong.

According to Veith, Mesmer believed that the healing powers of

> the magnetic fluid would be greatly enhanced if it were passed from him through, and to, many patients simultaneously. This "group practice" was attended by elaborate ceremony, which strongly appealed to the jaded tastes of his well-born patients in the French capital. The healing rituals took place in a heavily curtained room occupied by a large, covered wooden tub in the center. This tub, or *baquet*, was filled with water and magnetized iron filings. Jointed iron rods protruding through the pierced lid were directed by the patients to the ailing parts of their bodies. Mesmer made his appearance with the accompaniment of soft mournful music. He slowly passed among his patients, draped in a lavender-colored silken robe or suit, fixing his eyes upon each in turn and touching them with his hands or with a long magnetized iron wand, which he always carried with him.[4]

Occasionally the healing ceremonies were held outside under "magnetized" oak trees or on the banks of "magnetized" brooks or fountains. Beguiled by Mesmer's impressive ritual, the participants, predominantly women, fell into a somnolent trance or "mesmeric sleep," from which they awoke refreshed and healed.

Mesmer received hostile criticism from his medical colleagues, who succeeded in putting an end to Mesmer séances. Veith notes that public opposition persuaded Louis XVI to appoint a Royal Commission in 1784 to examine the validity of "ani-

---

[4]Veith, *Hysteria* (Chicago: University of Chicago Press, 1965), pp. 221-23.

mal magnetism." The group included such leading scientific personalities as Benjamin Franklin and Antoine Lavoisier. It was their judgment that Mesmer's cures were entirely due to imagination. When his practices were prohibited by the medical faculty of the University of Paris, Mesmer withdrew into obscurity. His ideas, however, never quite died out.

For our purposes it will be important to note two central features of these cults: ritual drama and the manipulation of something either in the body or in the mind. Anthropologist E. E. Evans-Pritchard has classified the features as characteristics of *sorcery*. Distinguishing sorcery from witchcraft, Evans-Pritchard defines the former as the power to manipulate and alter natural and supernatural events or states with the proper magical knowledge and performance of ritual. It is typically understood that the magic of sorcery can be put to good or bad use. Witchcraft, by contrast, is the possession of an inherited power and is used primarily for evil ends. Sorcerers depend on magic to implement their power, whereas witches derive their power from their mystical inheritance.[5] According to these definitions, we can conclude that most cults, including several recent new religions, are in fact systems of sorcery, or *magical religions*, and their leaders are modern-day sorcerers.

Of course we are not the first to reach this conclusion. Scholars such as Robin Horton have noted that sorcery, like religion, serves important philosophical and metaphysical functions for its practitioners. Horton argues that in the West sorcery serves much the same function that science serves. Both science and sorcery (and witchcraft and religion) are explanatory theories, at least in the sense that they reflect a quest "for unity underlying apparent diversity; for simplicity underlying apparent complexity; for order underlying apparent disorder; for regularity underlying apparent irregularity."[6]

But this modern confluence of magic, reason, science, and religion poses dangers of a sort. Paul Tournier was probably not wrong when he wrote about "the magic of Reason" and "the magic of Science." The spirit of magic, which in the new religions is often called spirituality and which our scholarly community is now trying to reclassify as altered states of consciousness in the

---

[5]See Evans-Pritchard, *Witchcraft, Oracles and Magic among the Azande* (London: Oxford University Press, 1937), pp. 8-11, 21-39.
[6]Horton, "African Traditional Thought and Western Science," in *Rationality*, ed. Bryan R. Wilson (Oxford: Blackwell, 1970), pp. 131-71.

context of a "transpersonal psychology," would appear to be in herent in human nature. Tournier defines magic as "the longing for the fairy tale, for the magic wand that will charm away the difficulties of life, the suffering, the limitations, and the uncertainties of our human condition."[7] Put more simply still, magic is the longing for simple solutions, for certitude. It is a condition to which idealistic middle-class youths are especially prone.

The fact that the distinction between science and reason on the one hand and magic and myth on the other is becoming ever more vague in our culture is a good indication that we—and our religions with us—are drifting toward faith in magic. It is Tournier's argument that the one holdout against this cultural tide is Christianity. He suggests that the key distinction is no longer between reason or magic, because reason itself is becoming magical as more and more people expect magical results from science. Rather, the key distinction is between all that is magical on the one hand and *faith* on the other.

HYSTERIA: CULTURAL CONDITION, RELIGIOUS CURE

There are some psychological conditions that even the layperson can recognize. It is the task of professional researchers to refine the questions and research methods necessary to pinpoint the problem more decisively. Sometimes the researchers fail and must redirect their attention to new avenues. Usually, when the condition they are studying is painful for the victims, those individuals will work as hard as the researchers to illuminate their condition and find a cure.

In Namibia, when Poewe was studying the Herero, she found that they kept directing her attention to their problems. They were racked by severe and unrelenting anxiety. They described themselves as oppressed by suspicion, deceit, and jealousy, as overcome by hopelessness, as dazed into stuporous indifference. Several women had very obvious symptoms that we associate with conversion hysteria. Many were hypochondriacs. Among the Herero, with their emphasis on seniority even among women, it was as if neurasthenia, hysteria, and hypochondria formed a continuum, the first two finding expression in the younger, the latter becoming fixed in the older population.

---

[7]Tournier, *A Doctor's Casebook in Light of the Bible*, trans. Edwin Hudson (New York: Harper & Row, 1960), pp. 118-20.

These findings suggest to us the existence of what might best be called a condition of *cultural hysteria* and a *hysterical culture*. We might define a hysterical culture as a culture of the oppressed and defeated—but a culture of the oppressed and defeated who cannot and will not accept defeat. They live with, and pass on to their children, a deep sense of moral injustice. Aching under the social imbalance with which they have to live, they become pre-occupied with their condition. They begin to perceive their fate as sacred. Suffering ties them to the transcendent. Spiritually open, they are very suggestible.

We might define cultural hysteria as the condition in which a people suffers from a sense of moral injustice so profound that their whole private and symbolic life comes to be centered on an *idee fixe*, a problem they can imagine being resolved only by an ultimate, dramatic, or sacred solution. The search for a sacred so-lution likewise makes the people peculiarly suggestible. The con-dition involves both social and psychological imbalances that may be further expressed in somatic or cultural imbalances. In some social settings the people may express their condition in dramatic somatic form (individual paralyses, inability to speak, blindness, localized aches and pains), or in equally dramatic psy-chological form (identity crises, transient psychoses, spirit pos-session, trance, or convulsions). In other social settings, the hys-teria may be expressed socially (in relationship imbalances, drifting, and such sociopathies as victimization, theft, and rescue or rape themes) or culturally (in suspicion, jealousy, death, chosen-people, and holocaust themes). Some or all such forms of expression may be present in any one society. Indeed, they may systematically reinforce or echo one another. Alternatively, in some societies only certain forms may be given expression, and then rather sporadically.

As Poewe has pointed out, the Herero defeat of 1904 was so severe that cultural hysteria became a universal phenomenon.[8] Among women, somatic and psychological expressions predomi-nate; among men, social expressions. Traugott K. Oesterreich makes a similar point about hysteria in relation to "the Jewish na-tion." Despite some scholarly suspicions that his work was preju-diced, there is reason to believe that some of his observations are significant.

Oesterreich, who had a Jewish wife and was dismissed by

---

[8]Poewe, *The Namibian Herero: A History of Their Psychosocial Disintegra-tion and Survival* (Lewiston, N.Y.: Edwin Mellen Press, 1985).

the Nazi government in 1933, wrote that "hysteria is numbered amongst the affections to which the Jewish nation is predisposed." He contends that this disposition toward hysteria originates not only from social relations but from deeper causes: "It is certain that life during the dispersion, the national conservatism of the Jews, the jealousy and ill-will called forth by the oppression of neighboring peoples and the feelings of permanent aversion resulting therefrom, contributed in many cases to produce and develop neuroses" that were socialized into succeeding generations.[9]

Three major elements of cultural hysteria—a deep sense of moral injustice, an *idee fixe*, and heightened suggestibility—are evident in new religions as well. For instance, we have already noted that an *idee fixe* is a key aspect of the four schismogeneses. In contemporary America, members of new religions consistently prove to be obsessed with some one aspect of their overall condition—an identity crisis, homosexual panic, wife battering or wife swapping, shoplifting or drug abuse, depression or emotional breakdown. We have noted such complaints in the case histories of Rajneeshies and members of the Unification Church in particular. More importantly, a long history of observations made by physicians indicates that such hysterical propensity to anger, suspicion, jealousy, and sad forebodings has always been a significant factor in a portion of our society and others. We noted earlier that the Herero experienced all of these reactions but felt particularly oppressed by suspicion and jealousy.

We also find the pattern of the hysterical personality in the case histories of those who have joined magical religions. The road to conversion to a new religion followed by middle-class youths in particular exemplifies this pattern. Individuals with hysterical personalities often describe interpersonal relationships that are "repetitive, impulsive, and stereotyped" along child-parent themes, rescue themes, or sometimes victim-aggressor themes. Personal testimonies of converts always include one or another of these themes. M. J. Horowitz studied the lives of such individuals for extended periods of time and noted especially the "frequent relationships in which the person fulfills a childlike role in relation to a caretaker, a waiflike role in relation to either an abandoning or rescuing person (ending with a recruiter of a new religion), and a helpless or sexually exploited

---

[9]Oesterreich, *Possession: Demoniacal and Others*, trans. D. Ibberson (New Hyde Park, N.Y.: University Books, 1966), pp. v, 171-72.

role in relation to an aggressor (a common theme among women who subsequently joined new religions)." Horowitz suggests that these persons must have a mental schemata or inner map that produces "fantasies and caricaturelike roles for self and others."[10]

Regarding the nature of the interpersonal relationships that hysterics are able to sustain, Horowitz suggests that they lead "drifting but possibly dramatic lives with an existential sense that reality is not really real."[11] Some say that they often feel as though they are not in control and not responsible, which in part explains their fascination with the occult. Many Rajneeshies, for example, describe having let the I Ching or chance meetings determine their next moves in life.

An assistant of ours who lived for a time among members of the Unification Church corroborated our observations of certain characteristics that Horowitz also describes—frequent "attention-seeking behavior," "displays of variable emotions," "behavioral provocativeness with self-recognition of intent," and, of course, "suggestibility." These features are found rarely in sociologists' analyses of members of new religions. When they are, it is typically because the sociologist has reproduced verbatim the accounts of the people interviewed. Participant observers are more likely to relate such findings, however.

Another category of characteristics that is typically omitted from sociological descriptions of members of new religions is short-term patterns of information processing. Sociologists simply aren't accustomed to making such relatively close observations. Nevertheless, some information of this sort is available to us. Horowitz made observations of behavior in small time intervals of minutes or seconds, and Bob Mullan's case histories give evidence of some of these characteristics, such as the use of language for effect on others rather than for meaning.[12] Experiential or magical religions almost seem to encourage "unclear verbal statements," "choice of global rather than specific labels for experience," and "failure to understand ideational implications," all of which tends to make members appear somewhat shallow.

It seems to us, then, that new religions are expressions of cultural hysteria. They amplify or produce hysterical tendencies

---

[10]Horowitz, "The Core Characteristics of Hysterical Personality," in *Hysterical Personality* (New York: Jason Aronson, 1977), pp. 3-6.

[11]Horowitz, "The Core Characteristics of Hysterical Personality," pp. 3-6.

[12]Mullan, *Life as Laughter* (London: Routledge & Kegan Paul, 1983), pp. 50-79.

at the same time that they "cure" them. And as we have seen, they are sought out by Westerners who display a Western form of hysterical personality. Hysteria is protean. It varies in its expression from culture to culture, from social class to social class, and from society to society. From earliest times it was characterized, quite correctly, as a spiritual or moral condition. To this day it is associated with those aspects of our social existence that create unjust distress and imbalance. The cure for cultural hysteria cannot be "normal" by definition, and when those who are afflicted with it cannot find relief in "normal" therapies, some turn to magical religions.

SOME DIFFERENCES BETWEEN CHRISTIANITY AND NEW RELIGIONS

One suspects that the real significance of the doctrine of justification by faith is no longer appreciated by many individuals in America's mainline churches and in the West generally. Steven M. Tipton has pointed out that mainline churches are increasingly pursuing what we judge to be a perverted path toward increasing emphasis on authority and obedience.[13] The social reaction of increased permissiveness and disaffection from mainline churches comes as no surprise. But the religious void that is being created is being filled not by a true religious revival, as Stark and Bainbridge contend,[14] but by a revival of *magical* religions.

One major distinction between Christianity and so-called new religions has to do with the difference between theistic *faith* and nontheistic *magic*. The distinction is not, it should be noted, between God on the one hand and faith in magic on the other. Faith in magic is a psychological impossibility. At most *belief* in magic may pacify suspicion, jealousy, and insecurity. But it cannot produce *faith*, because true faith excludes belief in magic. People who lose their faith often replace it almost unconsciously with belief in magic and intense allegiance to modern-day sorcerers or witches, individuals with "exemplary charisma" and "extraordinary personalities."

The belief in an acosmic monism, the oneness of all things, that pervades most new religions is far removed from the Chris-

---

[13]See Tipton, *Getting Saved from the Sixties: Moral Meaning in Conversion and Cultural Change* (Berkeley and Los Angeles: University of California Press, 1981), pp. 3-13, 253-61.
[14]See Stark and Bainbridge, *The Future of Religion*, pp. 116-20, 506-30.

tian understanding that there is a significant distinction between God and his creation. The two perspectives have profoundly different implications. Acosmic monism implies imminent magic, be it "inherited" as in witchcraft or subject to "manipulation" as in sorcery. The Christian distinction between God and his creation, on the other hand, implies the need for transcendent faith.

In keeping with their acosmic monism, most new religions advocate a mystical version of universal love and respect for all things. From this perspective, spontaneous and total self-expressiveness appears safe and even desirable. If all things are one, self-expressiveness is the proper cement with which to unite the community. In contrast, Christianity clearly distinguishes good from evil and maintains that there is a potential for either in all acts, beliefs, and attitudes. All self-expression is a matter of choice, and every choice entails a moral responsibility. It is naive to suppose that every choice we make, every way we choose to express ourselves, will necessarily be good.

The centrality of choice in Christianity has to do with what Arthur F. Holmes calls the *ad extra* of Christianity. All created things are *ad extra*—created by God "to the outside" of himself.[15] We noted, similarly, that the Bible suggests that the essence of marriage is the becoming of one flesh, and that children are not an indispensable element in this relationship: they are an extra. Holmes suggests that God gave the world its own reality and granted it delegated power and now cares for it with special acts of providence and miracles to achieve what otherwise would not occur. The fact that such providence is divinely added should discourage us from belief in magic. There is nothing intrinsic in the creation that will guide our destinies; *we* are responsible, and we must exercise our responsibility and choice.

Christianity stresses the fact that God has delegated power in creation, which underscores the limitations of human nature. New religions, on the other hand, tend to stress the exemplary charisma manifested by the extraordinary personality of their leaders. Christians refuse to worship individuals, although they respect them. The power of devotion to a charismatic leader invites worshipful imitation rather than the sorts of tough choices called for by a belief in delegated power.

[15]Holmes, *Contours of a World View*, Studies in a Christian World View, vol. 1 (Grand Rapids: Eerdmans, 1983), p. 64.

CHOOSE WHERE TO PLACE YOUR ANCHOR

It is unfortunate, though perhaps unavoidable, that much of the study of cults and new religions has been done by psychologists employing their standard medical model. We have tried to show that there are significant psycho-moral aspects of these new religions that this model cannot adequately account for, aspects that belong to the the sphere of religion or myth. Indeed, many individuals who join today's new religions solve their psychological and social problems in terms of fantasies derived from myths, some of which are derived from major religious and philosophical traditions. Such individuals perceive their psychological or social imbalances as deep social injustices that call for a dramatic and usually a moral or spiritual solution. As they translate their behavioral problems, emotional turmoil, and mental restlessness into fantasies or myths or, alternatively, as they translate myths into behavioral and emotional nuances, they undergo a "healing." So it is important that we take seriously not only the mythological fragments into which these searchers are hooking their anchors but also the officially sanctioned myth from which these fragments are breaking away or into which they are coalescing.

The essence of Christianity is trust. The essence of non-Western systems of witchcraft, sorcery, and divination is a mixture of mistrust, jealousy, and suspicion—precisely the opposite of trust. The centrality of trust in Christianity gives it a unique psychology, evident already in the story of Adam and Eve. When they fell, the bond of trust between God and humanity was broken, and we began to doubt God. Doubt and mistrust ravaged our psychology. We began to blame the evil we did on a vengeful or indifferent God. And yet no extent of efforts to free ourselves with such excuses is successful. As Hans Küng puts it, "compelled to justify himself, emancipated man attempts to exonerate himself, to find an alibi and to shift blame with the aid of a variety of excuse mechanisms. He practices the art of showing 'that it was not him.'"[16] We have attempted to blame evil on our environment, genetic pre-programming, our instinctive urges, "individual, social, linguistic structures," and in short on anything but ourselves.

Though we may be emancipated, we remain burdened with a nagging feeling of guilt. If emancipation cannot free us of guilt,

---

[16]Küng, *On Being a Christian* (London: Collins, 1978), pp. 429-30.

what can? Küng contends, and we agree, that the answer is re-demption. Redemption and emancipation both mean liberation, but whereas "emancipation means liberation of man by man . . . self-liberation,"[17] redemption means liberation of man by God, true liberation.

But how did, or how can, God redeem us? Through the birth and death of Christ. Christ was himself the God whom we learned to mistrust in the fall. To redeem us, God redeemed himself. He played out before our doubting eyes a beneficent act, his redemption, thereby redeeming us to a restored relationship of trust.

The story of redemption is simple—a God-man was born and died at our hands. But consider its implications. God entrusted us with his son, giving us the choice of which attitude we would assume toward him. We are subject to God, but we have freedom of choice nonetheless. What is more, the redemption teaches us not only that much of our suffering is self-inflicted, a consequence of lives lived in mistrust, but it also teaches us how difficult it is to restore a relationship: it entails creating a new sense of trust. Trust, not mystical merging, is what cements relationships and clears our minds. And further still, in freeing us of the burden of guilt that results from our collective heinous acts, God restores our sense of proportion. In the process of redeeming us, the resurrection distinguishes us from God, redefines us as finite but free. God's revelation of his infinity frees us from the delusion that we are or ever can be gods. Exhilarated by the wholesome clarity of mind these insights afford us, we can be, in the words of H. A. Meynell, "unrestrictedly attentive, intelligent and reasonable" as we explore ourselves, the world, and the universe.[18] We need pause in this quest only to make certain that we have chosen the good rather than the bad, that we remain grounded in our trust in God.

[17]Küng, *On Being a Christian*, p. 430.
[18]Meynell, *The Intelligible Universe* (New York: Barnes & Noble, 1982), p. 115.

Index

Index

Index   **169**

Pappenheim, Bertha, 144-145
Personality disorders, 142, 144, 147, 152
Plato, 25
Poewe, Karla, 101, 105, 136, 159-60
Prabhupada, Swami, 74, 75, 83
Primal experiences: and case histories, 62-72; and coincidences, 66; definition of, 60; in England, 61; and hysteria, 144; and new mythology, 63; and new religions, 98, 131; and peak experiences, 24; as psychotherapeutic, 104; and shamans, 132, 146; in the United States, 61
Psychotherapy, 113, 147

Rajneesh, Bhagwan Shree, 100, 113, 135
Rajneesh movement, 99, 100, 112, 113, 114, 115, 120, 122, 146
Reiser, Judy, 30
Richardson, James T., 6, 7
Roszak, Theodore, 43, 44

St. Francis of Assisi, 23
Sargant, William: and brainwashing, 8; and fundamentalists, 9
Schismogenesis, 103, 105, 106-10, 120, 130, 152, 161
Schizoid conditions, 105, 106
Schizophrenia, 142
Science fiction fantasy, 29, 30, 33, 37, 71
Scientific worldview, 19, 20
Scientology, 129, 157
Sects, 127-29
Shaker community, 135
Shaman, 137, 138, 139-40, 144, 145, 150
Shamanism, 80; in China, 138; and group therapy, 138; in Japan, 138, 140, 141; and new

religions 139, 145; and self-training, 137; and transient psychosis, 141, 142
Shamanistic religions, 131, 132, 136, 141
Shirokogoroff, S. M., 145
Sinclair, Alex, 152
Smart, Ninian, 74
Smith, Joseph, Jr., 39, 40, 56, 135, 139
Somatic disorders, 136, 144, 160
Spangler, David, 38, 44, 78
Spirit possession, 132, 134, 140-44; and cultural hysteria, 160
Stark, Rodney, 116; and compensators, 154; and market model, 117

Thaumaturgical sects, 128
Therapo-moral cults, 47, 155-57
Thompson, William Irwin, 44-45
Tillich, Paul, 15, 16
Tipton, Steven, M., 81, 89, 105-6, 117-19
Tolkien, J. R. R., 38, 71
Tournier, Paul, 158, 159
Transcendental Meditation, 154-55
Transpersonal ties, 113, 114, 120
Trobisch, Walter, 121

UFOs, 32-33, 36
Unification Church, 37, 100, 112, 114, 115; and primal experiences, 98, 99, 145-46; and reformist movement, 130

Veith, Ilza, 151, 153, 156, 157

Wallace, Anthony, 127
Wallis, Roy, 117
Watson, Lyall, 31-32
Wilson, Bryan, 6-7, 116, 117, 124, 127
Witchcraft, 151, 158
Wittgenstein, Ludwig, 15
Wuthnow, Robert, 61